THE LIFE
OF
RICHARD
CADBURY

Cover Images:

This was a chocolate box design originally painted by Richard Cadbury that also featured on the cover of *Cadbury's Angels* by Iris Carrington. (*Reproduced with kind permission from the family*)

Richard and Emma Cadbury surrounded by all of Richard's children. (back) Barrow, Edith, Richard Jr, William, Margaret, Richard. (front) Helen, Beatrice, Jessie, Emma. (*Reproduced with kind permission from the family*)

Richard with his youngest daughter, Beatrice, 1890. (*Reproduced with kind permission from the family*)

The almshouses in Bournville today. (© *Ian Wordsworth*)

Richard Cadbury 1835 – 1899, from a painting by Percy Bigland, June 1925. (*No copyright restrictions known. Used with permission from Richard Cadbury's great-granddaughter Mary Penny*)

THE LIFE
OF
RICHARD CADBURY

SOCIALIST, PHILANTHROPIST & CHOCOLATIER

DIANE WORDSWORTH

PEN & SWORD
HISTORY

AN IMPRINT OF PEN & SWORD BOOKS LTD.
YORKSHIRE – PHILADELPHIA

First published in Great Britain in 2020 by
PEN AND SWORD HISTORY
An imprint of
Pen & Sword Books Ltd
Yorkshire – Philadelphia

ISBN 978 1 52676 825 4

A CIP catalogue record for this book is available from the British Library.

Typeset in Times New Roman 11.5/14 by
SJmagic DESIGN SERVICES, India.
Printed and bound in the UK by TJ Books Ltd.

Pen & Sword Books Limited incorporates the imprints of Atlas, Archaeology,
Aviation, Discovery, Family History, Fiction, History, Maritime, Military,
Military Classics, Politics, Select, Transport, True Crime, Air World,
Frontline Publishing, Leo Cooper, Remember When, Seaforth Publishing,
The Praetorian Press, Wharncliffe Local History, Wharncliffe Transport,
Wharncliffe True Crime and White Owl.

For a complete list of Pen & Sword titles please contact
PEN & SWORD BOOKS LIMITED
47 Church Street, Barnsley, South Yorkshire, S70 2AS, England
E-mail: enquiries@pen-and-sword.co.uk
Website: www.pen-and-sword.co.uk

Or
PEN AND SWORD BOOKS
1950 Lawrence Rd, Havertown, PA 19083, USA
E-mail: Uspen-and-sword@casematepublishers.com
Website: www.penandswordbooks.com

Contents

Acknowledgements

I would like to thank the following for their help and kindness while I was researching this book: Lydia Dutton and family for allowing us to take photographs of the plaque on the front of their house; Mary Penny, Richard Cadbury's great-granddaughter, who made a wonderful and hard-working research assistant; Melissa Atkinson and the team in the library at Friends House in London; Bettina Gray and the library staff at Woodbrooke College in Birmingham; Aileen Pringle at Pen & Sword for all of her advice and especially her patience; and photographer, chauffeur and chief supporter, my husband Ian Wordsworth.

Foreword

I grew up in Bournville, the village created by George Cadbury. In winter, the promise of snow was heralded by the smell of chocolate. It came from the factory, dear to the heart of the 'other' Cadbury brother, Richard.

As a granddaughter of Richard's son William, and William's wife Emmeline, I am very grateful to Diane Wordsworth for her testimony to this 'kind and interesting man', which has brought alive many of the memories and traditions of the 'Richard Cadbury' family.

Beside me as I write is a vase of bright blue gentians, memories of the Switzerland Richard loved. Gentians always grew in William and Emmeline's garden, where the summer house was built like a Swiss chalet, toboggans and skis stored in the loft. Each year, on Good Friday, Hot Cross Buns continue to flourish in the gardens of Richard's descendants.

His concern for the health, social and spiritual welfare of women has also passed through the generations. Richard gave the first address at the Women's Monday Meeting in Stirchley. The men of his adult school had asked for something for their wives, too busy at home to attend on a Sunday. The meeting was conducted by Emma and her daughters, my grandmother Emmeline, my mother and, on occasion, by me. It closed in 1984.

Perhaps the most poignant memory is the olive wood Jerusalem desk bought at the time of Richard's death. William Cadbury had travelled with a nurse to be with his father, but rough seas prevented landing. The endless card games played in anguished waiting live on in the family as 'Joppa Patience'.

Richard's particular contribution to Bournville was the building of the Almshouses. As a child, the Almshouse party was a Christmas highlight, and it always snowed! Beneath the portraits of Richard and

Emma, long decorated tables were set up and Christmas dinner arrived from the factory kitchens. Richard's grandsons carved the turkeys, while dishes of vegetables steamed by the blazing fire. Feasting done, the entertainment arrived, with excited great-grandchildren corralled and costumed, ready for performance.

As in Richard's time, the party ended with prayers, and with this carol, which begins:

As with gladness, men of old
Did the guiding star behold.

This book brings you a life of joy and gladness, a life lived in the Spirit, and guided by the star.

Mary Penny
October 2020

Chapter 1

Background in brief

Richard Tapper Cadbury was the founder of the Birmingham branch of the Cadbury family. He was born in Exeter on 6 November 1768 and was apprenticed at the age of 14 to William Chandler of Strood in Kent. This apprenticeship was cut short at the end of the American War of Independence (1775 – 1783), when returning soldiers found themselves unable to pay their debts and Mr Chandler could no longer pay his own bills. From Strood Richard Tapper was apprenticed to a Gloucester draper named James White, where he stayed until the age of 21.

Richard's next post was in London with silk mercer and linen draper Jasper Capper, whose business was later taken over by Robinson and Cleaver. During Richard Tapper's stay in London, he met Joseph Rutter, and in 1794 the pair visited Birmingham. This was Richard's first visit to Birmingham, but Joseph had been there before. The two friends went to a Friends' meeting in Bull Street and later rented the premises at 92 Bull Street (originally numbered 85). Four years later, Joseph left the partnership to join his brother in London, and the business transferred to the sole name of Richard T. Cadbury.

On 5 October 1796, Richard married Elizabeth Head in Ipswich. At first they lived in Old Square in Birmingham, where three of their children – Sarah, Benjamin Head and Joel – were born. The family then moved to accommodation over the shop in Bull Street, where the rest of their children – Maria, John, James, Ann, Jesse, Emma Joel – were born. Another Emma was born in 1808 but died in 1809. Emma Joel was born in 1811.

When Richard Tapper Cadbury was 60 years old, he retired to Calthorpe Road, near Five Ways in Edgbaston. He died on 13 March 1860 at the ripe old age of 91. Many sources say he was 92, but as his birthday was in November, he was still 91. Either way, it was still a good age.

John Cadbury was Richard Tapper Cadbury's third son, the second of his children born at the Bull Street property. In 1816, John was apprenticed to John Cudworth of Broadhead and Cudworth in Briggate, Leeds. It was here that he learnt about the retail business and tea dealing. In 1822, he went to London to gain more experience, and he returned to Birmingham a year later.

Upon his return, John's father gave him some money with which he could 'sink or swim', and on 4 March 1824, John used the money to open his first shop at 93 Bull Street, next door to his father's draper's business. Alongside tea and coffee John also sold cocoa beans. In 1831, John moved his business to a factory in Crooked Lane. As this was when the actual manufacture of chocolate was begun, it is also considered to be the foundation of the Cadbury business we know today.

John's older brother Benjamin Head Cadbury joined the firm in 1847, and the business became known as Cadbury Brothers. They were joined in the company by two of John's sons, Richard in 1850 and George in 1856. Their younger brother Henry joined the firm in 1869, but sadly died in 1875 at the age of only 30. Benjamin Head Cadbury retired in 1860.

In 1826, John married Priscilla Dymond of Exeter. Priscilla's brother was John's friend Jonathan, a Quaker essayist and philosopher who wrote *Essays on the Principles of Morality*. Richard Cadbury was later to become close friends with one of Jonathan's sons, and Maria Cadbury, his sister, went to a boarding school run by Mary, Miriam and Josephine Dymond. Sadly, within two years of the marriage, Priscilla had died. It was during the lonely years that followed Priscilla's death that John Cadbury threw himself into public affairs and Society of Friends' activities.

During his sister Sarah's engagement to John Barrow, a woollen draper from Lancaster, John Cadbury met Barrow's sister, Candia. At the time, Candia was still only 15 and John Cadbury had not yet completed his apprenticeship. So, despite admiring her greatly, any kind of romantic relationship was out of the question. However, they met again, four years after he was widowed, and they married after all in 1832.

At first, John and Candia lived over the Bull Street shop where their first child John was born. They moved to Frederick Road in Edgbaston in 1834, and Richard was born in 1835. Richard was followed by a sister and three younger brothers.

John Cadbury continued to attend meetings up until two Sundays before his death. But he had caught a chill and he died on 11 May 1889. He was 88.

Chapter 2

Childhood and growing up

Richard Cadbury was born on 29 August 1835 at Frederick Road in Edgbaston. He was John and Candia Cadbury's second son. The house at 17 Frederick Road was temporary until John Cadbury could move the family from the townhouse in Bull Street. Soon after Richard was born, the family moved to Calthorpe Road, where they remained for the next forty years. Maria, George, Edward and Henry were born here, as well as another brother who only lived for a few days. At first, the house was not really considered large enough for such a big family and Richard's sister Maria described it as 'almost cottage-like'. But it had a nice garden and was surrounded by countryside, and the house was extended and added to over the years.

Richard Cadbury and his four brothers and their sister had a happy, idyllic childhood. They were brought up strictly, as per the Puritan Quaker tradition, but they were surrounded by trees and the boys had a couple of ponies to ride, though as there were no stable-boys, the children had to look after the horses themselves. The brothers would race around the countryside on their ponies and were often reported to their parents for 'furious riding'. The family didn't keep a carriage and horses, preferring instead to walk everywhere.

Candia Barrow came from Lancaster, and Richard's Aunt Sarah had also already married into the Barrow family at the time of John and Candia's wedding. The children would therefore often visit their relations in Lancaster. The mail van picked them up in Preston and dropped them off not far from the garden gate. Their maternal grandfather, George Barrow, owned several farms along the border with Yorkshire.

Although the garden was mostly under their mother's care, the children had their own plots in which to play and learn. There was a small pond with a rockery island in the middle and a fountain, surrounded by ferns. Richard's particular responsibility were the ferns and the water plants. Sweet nectarines and juicy peaches grew on trees against the walls whilst there were luscious lawns on which to exercise and play games, with gymnastic poles for climbing. Their father, John, apparently measured the garden and decided that twenty-one times around the lawn equalled a mile, and the children had to run this distance each morning before breakfast, chasing their hoops. Often Richard would show off and run a mile and a half. They went on long walks with their dogs too. Sometimes the children would accompany their father on his walk around the countryside at 7.00 am prompt. Breakfast was at 8.00 am, and at 9.00 am their father was dressed and ready for work.

Maria Cadbury, the only daughter, wrote:

> *Our home was one of sunshine. Our parents doing all they could to make us happy, and the consistency of their own lives was a great help in forming the characters and tastes of their children. Home was the centre of attraction to us all, and simple home pleasures our greatest joy.*
>
> (*Appendix I*)

The children also had Jew's harps to play and they enjoyed singing. In fact, their mother would sing to them as well and when they were old enough, they accompanied their parents to the Friends' Meeting House in Bull Street, Birmingham, for weekly worship.

Richard and his brother John were initially taught by a governess at home. Her name was Martha Heath and she lived fairly close to them. Richard's daughter, Helen, later wrote:

> *He and his brother John were devoted to her. She lived quite near their home in Frederick Road. One day, when Richard was about three years old, an active little fellow, with fair curly hair, his grandfather came unexpectedly upon him, toddling alone across the road, and took him home. It was discovered that the little lad had slipped out of the house unnoticed, and was on his way to visit his "dear governess."*
>
> (*Richard Cadbury of Birmingham*)

At the age of 6, Richard went to a very well-known Friends' day school in Birmingham run by William Lean. He was joined by his cousin Thomas Barrow from Lancaster, who stayed at the Cadbury home while he studied in Birmingham. By the time Richard was 7, his older brother John had already moved on to boarding school, and Richard wrote him a letter dated 1842 that gives some idea of the toys the children played with and the language still in use in the mid-nineteenth century:

> *MY DEAR BROTHER, – I have got a railway train, first, second, and third-class carriages, with an engine and tender; this was a present from my dear papa. Wilt thou send me a letter with some sweet violets for dear mamma? she* [sic] *is so fond of them. Grandmother sends her love to thee. I got some pictures and send some of them to thee, they are so pritty* [sic].
>
>

I am thy affectionate brother,
RICHARD CADBURY.

When Richard was almost aged 8, he joined his older brother John at boarding school. The boarding school was at Charlbury, near to the Wychwood Forest in the Cotswolds. The head teacher was Miss Maria Palmer, who was a strict disciplinarian, but the kind-hearted deputy head teacher, Mary Lamb, tried to relieve the boys' homesickness. A coach took them to the school, driving through the towns and villages of Stratford-on-Avon and Shipston-on-Stour to Enstone, where they were met and taken on to Charlbury. On Sundays they were able to attend the local meeting run by some very old-fashioned Quakers.

A schoolfriend of Richard's at the time remembered a funny story from those days, where there are more clues about how the family lived back in Birmingham:

> *The summer holidays were over, and a new suit of clothes for little John Cadbury, which had not been sent home in time, was forwarded to him at Charlbury School. It was early in August, and the luscious gooseberries in the Edgbaston home garden were ripe. The clothes had been packed in one of the long, narrow hampers, used for fish, which were usually very flimsy, and the good father, always wanting to share home pleasures with his boys at school, filled the basket up with gooseberries. [...] As the hamper had to travel fifty miles on the top of the coach, and had*

then to be carried three miles on the back of the unfortunate country postman, you can imagine what happened. The postman, poor man, said the juice had been running down his back all the way, and his coat was soaked through. The condition of the new suit of clothes was something tragic, and I believe they had to go into the wash-tub. It was very comical, and Maria Palmer and Mary Lamb laughed so heartily over it, that it was fixed on my memory.

(Richard Cadbury of Birmingham)

As if to confirm the incident, and as well as to send news from home, John Cadbury wrote a letter to the boys, dated 18 August 1843:

MY DEAR JOHN AND RICHARD, – Your dear mother gathered for you a basket of fine, ripe gooseberries, which were sent by coach yesterday; we hope you and your schoolfellows have enjoyed them by this time. I am glad to say your mother is very finely. Edward grows fast; Maria and George delight to be with him. They are very well and often talk of you. Next week I expect they will go to school in Bath Row to a Friend, and your cousins Joel and Mary are to go to the same school. We were very glad to hear that you were both comfortably settled and happy. I am sure you will be, if you use your best efforts to please your governess, and in all things do as she wishes. In the basket will also be found light waistcoats for John, which mother thinks will be very pleasant wear this hot weather. I still intend paying you a short visit, perhaps next month, and as the time draws nearer shall write the exact time. In all things love one another – be kindly affectionate to one another. Our dear love to you both. Your dear grandparents, uncles, and aunts are well, and send their love.

Letters from their mother reminded the boys to do their duties. A paper written by Richard when he was still only 8 recorded these duties:

A mother's affectionate desire for her precious child,
    Every morning before you leave your room – wash yourselves clean, brush your hair very tidily, also your teeth,

6

put your clothes neatly – *let your hearts rise to God in grateful feelings for preserving you through the night, desiring that He will be with you through the day, to keep you from every wrong thought and action, preserving you in love to each other, and to all in the house and everywhere. These feelings will help you through all your difficulties and trials, remembering that His Almighty eye is upon you and sees all your strivings, and hears all your prayers to conquer that cruel and selfish spirit, which is always ready to crush all our good desires. January 15th, 1844, RICHARD CADBURY, JUNR.*

(*Richard Cadbury of Birmingham*)

Whenever the boys returned home from school, their brother George and sister Maria looked forward to seeing them again. The other brothers, Edward and Henry, were still very young at this time. Maria wrote:

It was a real gala day to my brother George and myself when John and Richard came home for the holidays. I remember one summer day our standing at the nursery window, with large crimson peonies in our hands, watching for the coach which brought them home from Charlbury, as the railway was not then completed. We had happy holidays, and enjoyed working in our own gardens; we liked helping to gather fruit, also to top and tail gooseberries and shell peas, seeing who could fill a basin first. The boys were allowed to make supplies of pop, and very good it was, with a piece of bread and cheese.

(*Richard Cadbury of Birmingham*)

When Richard was 11 years old he stayed home from boarding school for a few months due to ill health – it is not recorded what ailed him. He didn't get off that lightly though, and still had to attend school locally. Nor did he avoid attending meetings. On 28 September 1845, he wrote to his brother John, who by now had started at school in Hitchin:

MY DEAR BROTHER, – We are very much obliged for thy kind letters, which thou hast sent us. On Fourth Day

[Wednesday] *I and father went to Dudley Monthly Meeting; we went there in a good-sized car and two horses. After Meeting we went to dinner at Edward Williams; we went all round his garden, and there was a beautiful pond with some gold-fish in it; he has two little girls, and I met them carrying three little puppies, which were very pretty; after dinner we went to John Williams, where there was a great many little children running about. After we had been there a little while we went to see Dudley Castle, and went all about it. We met a man on the way that told us something about it; after that we went to tea at R.H. Smith's. After tea we got ready and jumped on the car and came home to Birmingham. I sent thy letters off to George and Maria on Third Day* [Tuesday]. *I very often think of thee and wonder how thou gets on. I went with Charlotte this morning to the other garden, and we picked up all the apples that had fallen. I remain,*

Thy affectionate brother,
RICHARD CADBURY.

During his time of convalescence, Richard felt a responsibility towards his younger siblings. Maria and George were aged 7 and 8; Edward and Henry were still toddlers. Their mother's room had a small room off it and here, on Sunday afternoons, Richard would read aloud to the two oldest children. This was followed by a short time of prayer. When the weather was more clement, this little meeting took place outside in the arbour in the garden.

Of course, the children didn't only have Cadbury grandparents. Their mother Candia Barrow had parents too and childhood visits were also made to the children's grandfather in Lancaster. Behind his house was a tower where they could watch the many sea vessels returning from their sea voyages. Some of the ships even belonged to their grandfather.

Candia owned a farmhouse on Ingleborough variously called 'Skalemire' and sometimes 'Skalemire Castle' or 'Scalemire' in family records and documents. It had belonged to her father, George Barrow. When he died in 1842, it passed to his oldest daughter, and the family enjoyed holidaying there. The walls of this farmhouse were 3 feet thick in places and the land went to almost the top of Ingleborough. Here the children learnt about life on the farm and how to appreciate nature.

Richard completed his convalescence at his mother's farm on Ingleborough, and in the spring of 1846, he was sent to Hitchin in Hertfordshire to a school run by Benjamin Abbott. He literally swapped places with his brother John, who had hurt his leg and was recovering at home. His first letter home from Hitchin was dated 20 March 1846:

> *MY VERY DEAR PARENTS, – I am sorry that I have not wrote to you for so long. I am very much obliged for your kind letter. I have been to a lecture twice; one was about Bethliem* [sic] *and the other about Jerusellm* [sic]. *[...] There is one day scholar, G. Latchmore, and two of master's sons, Arthur Abbot and Aston Abbot. I feel very comfortable, and I think John will when he has been here a little while. I am very much obliged for Maria's note, and I intend to send her one in return for it. Please give my dear love to all. I remain,*
>
> > *Thy affectionate son,*
> > *R. CADBURY.*

A letter that was dated 23 March 1846 from John Cadbury must have crossed with Richard's letter home. John wrote:

> *MY DEAR RICHARD, – Thy sister is anxious her letter should go. I will therefore add a few lines to tell thee that thy dear mother, sweet little Henry and Edward, also George, Maria and John, are well, and all have much love to send thee. John goes to W. Lean's at seven in the morning and stays all day. His leg is fast getting well. We hope to hear from thee very soon; thou canst tell us who are thy playfellows, who sleeps in thy room, how thou manages with thy lessons, and whether thou feels happy and settled. We often talk about thee, and when we sat round the fire last evening, each repeating a few verses, and then a little serious conversation and reading, our hearts overflowed in affectionate remembrance of thee; yes, my dear boy, it may*

*be said the greater the distance from us, the closer the tie
of love and solicitude. Be a good boy, be diligent and very
attentive, strive in all things to spare giving thy master
trouble, "Remember thy Creator in the days of thy youth."*

By July 1846, Richard had been rejoined at school by his brother, John,
but in November of that year, Richard was at home again. He wrote to
John on 23 November 1846:

*MY VERY DEAR BROTHER, – Thou art having great
advantages in being at school, whilst I have so very little
schooling, that I fear thou wilt get a long way before me,
especially in Latin. I have been out this morning with notes,
to invite some friends to meet Joseph Sturge and his bride
to tea at our house. Our little dog "Trim" very often goes
out with father and me before breakfast, and on Sixth Day
morning [Friday] we had a violent storm of wind and rain,
which frightened him so much, that he ran howling to a
person's door, and laid with his dirty feet upon the step,
which so enraged the gardener, that he kicked him up like a
football, which almost drove him out of his senses, and he
ran into the very next house, making a dreadful noise, so as
to frighten all the neighbourhood, so that we were obliged
to carry him all the way home. The same day I had another
disaster, that of taking my kitten to town to live; when she
came out of the basket, she came spinning out like a top,
and continued to whirl for some time, and then lay down
as if she were dead, but she has recovered, and has settled
down quite well ever since. Accept a great deal of love for
thyself, from thy affectionate brother,*

RICHARD CADBURY

*P.S. – Please do not forget to give my love to Master and
Mistress Dina Abbot, and any of the boys that would like to
have it.*

A few years later, in 1847, Trim the dog was mentioned in dispatches
again, this time by Candia in a letter to Richard: *Poor Trim has had an*

accident. In peeping under the large gates a dog outside seized his nose, and would not loose his hold until severely flogged. Trim has recovered from it, but is much annoyed with it. He has a walk most mornings with your dear father.

While Richard and John were at school in Hitchin, the family were concerned with the famine in Ireland. About a million people are believed to have died in Ireland from 1846 to 1851, due to starvation and related epidemic conditions, while another million fled to America and Great Britain. The fungus, known as potato blight (*Phytophthora infestans* or *P. infestans*), first struck in 1845 and half of the potato crop was ruined. Over the next seven years, three-quarters of the crop was lost. On 4 February 1847, Maria wrote to her brothers: *I am sorry I could not write to you before, because I have been making clothes for the poor Irish.*

A few days later, on 12 February, their mother Candia wrote to the boys, and this letter provides information on how Richard had recently been spending his free time:

MY DEAR JOHN AND RICHARD, – Since I last wrote we have been gratified and cheered by receiving several letters from you. We have thought of our dear Richard in his walks during the winterly, snowy weather we have had for more than a week. The thermometer has been 12° below freezing. [...] We are still engaged in sending off money and clothes to Ireland. I wish they may reach the most destitute. Many benevolent people in that country are giving up their time to assist the poor wretched sufferers. May we who are spared such distress endeavour to cultivate thankful hearts to Him from whom all our blessings flow, by endeavouring to live up to His precepts and divine will. I have often thought of you with prayerful desires that you might be permitted to have your minds rightly engaged in Meeting to seek for renewed strength to do your duty, remembering that nothing can prosper without the blessing of the Almighty upon it, and that whatever we do, we should do all to His glory. We know not how soon we may be called to account for our thoughts and actions in Meeting as well as elsewhere.

Your affectionate mother.

Their father always ensured the boys had a piece of home with them while they were away at school, and his letters reveal the kinds of things that the family grew in the gardens. On 4 March 1847, John wrote:

MY DEAR BOYS, – A basket goes to-day to the car of W. Manby, to be forwarded to you, I hope to-morrow, by the carrier. It contains two drums of figs, and another drum, the largest, contains oranges at the top, and the cake at the bottom, which I have cut up for you ready for use, and you must therefore be careful how you open it. The fourth drum also contains oranges, and in the string at the top of one of them is a small parcel for John from his mother, brother, and sister. Now I should think if you divide one drum *of figs amongst the boys it will do, and then perhaps you can give to your particular friends the rest. We were pleased to receive John's note and* commend *him for not being made the tool of others to do what is wrong – let others do what they may, but do you, dear boys, in all things do what you know to be right. Let boys do their own wrong deeds, you do right not to be made the cat's-paw of any. We all keep finely, and all send their love to you. Write as soon as you get the basket, and tell us how you get on with its contents.*

Your affectionate father.

It is not recorded what the other boys had been up to, and John's letter to his parents has not survived, but it is refreshing to know that boys will be boys, whatever the era.

Although Richard was fond of exercise and sport, he was not particularly strong. Therefore, instead of having lessons before breakfast with the other boys at school, John Cadbury arranged for him to have long walks in the surrounding countryside. The family strongly believed that fresh air and exercise in pleasant surroundings was exceptionally good for the health and wellbeing, but they ensured that Richard understood that his morning walks were also a privilege. Caleb R. Kemp was a schoolfriend of Richard's. He remembered: *I was at school with him at Benjamin Abbot's at Hitchin, and he was a good-tempered and very pleasant schoolfellow. He was not in strong health, and did no work before breakfast, but took a country walk instead.*

This enforced country activity gave Richard a great love of natural history, and he would bring back all manner of interesting objects and curiosities. He collected butterflies, birds' eggs, insects, and so on. Richard had never met his cousin Joel, but when Joel wrote to him from America, it seems that he sent his cousin yet more collectibles:

MY DEAR COUSIN, – Hearing thou was interested in the collection of English insects, moths, and butterflies, I thought a few specimens from our country would not be unacceptable, though the manner of preserving them be different from that practised by you. I hope it will not debar them from entrance into thy collection. Thy loving, but unknown cousin,
JOEL CADBURY.

In the summer of 1847, a friend was able to join Richard on these early morning walks. Candia Cadbury wrote on 3 August:

I find by thy master's letter that he is so kind as to find a companion for dear Richard in his morning walks. Now I am anxious my dear boy should show his gratitude by endeavouring to do all his kind caretakers wish him to do, and still to feel that he is the responsible person, when out; not to do anything they may disapprove of, and to return at the right time. *His good conduct in this respect has gained him their confidence, and now I hope he will keep it with his increased privilege.*

John Cadbury confirmed this company on Richard's walks when he wrote, on 7 August: *We hope Richard's walks will, now he has a companion, be more enjoyable to him, but be sure not in any way to presume or encroach on the liberty so allowed.*

The school holidays were quite different in those days, and Richard was often back at school by the time his birthday came around. His mother wrote to him on 28 August 1849, to ensure he knew he hadn't been forgotten:

MY VERY DEAR RICHARD, – This is to meet thee upon thy attaining thy fourteenth birthday; as we cannot meet to congratulate thee upon the event we must be satisfied to do so by writing, and be assured we all feel most affectionately interested with warm desires for thy progress in the right path. I do not know whether thou continues thy practice of lying down each day; if thou does I think it would afford thee a quiet opportunity of reading of the text for the day in the little book Aunt Benjamin gave thee; it might sometimes be a help and strength to thee to do right. Thy fern is putting out its fronds most beautifully, and the one we brought from Scalemire two years since is looking strong and well. I intend to mark it, that we may more easily find it another time. Thou hast our united and affectionate wishes for thy future happiness and good.

At this time, many diseases and illnesses were common and in the autumn of 1849, there was a serious international outbreak of cholera. On 13 September 1849, Candia wrote to Richard and John:

[...] So thankful that you were "both quite well," *for which I assure you I felt truly thankful, and my heart almost leapt for joy when I read it. With thankful feelings I can report the same of all our family and families, and indeed all north of the town; at least, the medical men at the hospital say that we have not any more illness than is usual here at the time of year.*

This was followed by another letter dated 22 September:

[...] Yesterday was kept as a fast by the people of Birmingham, to thank the Almighty for His goodness in sparing them from cholera, and to pray for His continued preservation from this fearful visitation. I should think all places of worship were open, the shops closed, and all business suspended. We have indeed cause for great thankfulness in being so lightly dealt with. May we live more continually in the remembrance of it.

In the spring of 1850, John left school to join the business while Richard returned alone, although it appears from correspondence that John had

14

a period of poor health at this time. In April, the family went away on holiday to Malvern, but they did not forget poor Richard who was stuck at school on his own. On 9 April 1850, Candia wrote to her son:

> [...] *Father now hopes John may be well enough to return with him next week to go into Bull Street entirely [...] Edward and Henry are in great delight with the beautiful flowers they find – sweet violets and primroses in abundance, Henry running from one bunch to another, not knowing which to admire most, culling them and bringing them home in the full glee and happiness of his little brother.*

Later that summer, on 29 August, Richard spent his fifteenth birthday away from the family. Richard was to receive two letters from his father in short succession:

> [A few days after his birthday] MY DEAR RICHARD, – *We were not unmindful of thy birthday on Fifth Day, and many were the good wishes that passed our lips, none more affectionately desiring thy happiness than thy father and mother. Fifteen years have soon rolled over, time passed that can never return. The time to come none can tell beyond the present moment, so that we are called on to "Let the day's work keep pace with the day" – to-morrow may not be ours. Eternity stands before us, so that, my dear boy, we are most anxious thou should in every way improve the moments as they speed along. We have a parcel waiting to send thee. I continue to take Trim and Sappho a walk in the morning, much to their joy and benefit. Sappho very kindly, a few days ago, pulled Trim up by his neck, and carrying him into the pond, gave him several dips and then let him go; it amused us all very much. We begin to think how pleasant it will be to have thy help to work with and for us. John is very steady at his post in Bull Street. The garden is still gay with flowers of every hue. Yesterday we cut a delicious melon, and have an ample supply of fine cucumbers.*

> [On 10 September] *A parcel containing thy birthday cakes is sent off to-night. (Presents also from John, George, Maria*

and Edward.) It also has a nice copy of the Holy Scriptures enclosed, which is a joint present from thy father and mother. We trust it may prove a lasting comfort, pleasure, and profit to thee in the best sense. A little time spent each day in its private *perusal cannot fail to do good, and we desire to encourage thee through every discouragement to persevere in this habit of daily reading, and silently meditating on what thou reads. The mind is thus often attracted to the divine source from whence alone all good must come. "Seek and ye shall find; ask and ye shall receive"; these are blessed promises, and may be realised this day as much as at the time they were given forth by our adorable and blessed Redeemer, but we must all remember He is alone the way, the truth, and life. Thy affectionate father.*

Richard, as a 15-year-old boy, must have been thrilled with that gift from his parents. He stayed at Hitchin until he was almost 16, finally leaving school in the summer of 1851. While the older boys were away at school, both at Charlbury and then Hitchin, the younger children remained at home to be taught by a governess.

Their mother Candia had a recipe book and inside it could be found methods for preserving various fruits, how to make crab apple jelly and recipes for country wines. The boys made ginger beer and John Cadbury Sr was known for his barley pudding demonstrations at temperance meetings – as an alternative use of barley usually meant for booze.

John and Candia Cadbury were total abstainers and the family were brought up to be the same. Maria remembered:

It was not easy in those early days of the Temperance Society for our parents to give up offering wine and other spirituous drinks to their friends, for it was looked on as a mark of want of hospitality, and even the family circle did not at first approve of it. Our parents both worked hard in visiting the families of drunkards; and we always liked going with either of them. Our father signed the pledge with Joseph Livesey at the first meeting held in Birmingham in 1832. He built a room for temperance meetings, and had them sometimes

16

filled with drunkards. Two splendid men arose from those meetings who became very attractive platform speakers in the cause of total abstinence. They were both Birmingham blacksmiths, Thomas Barlow and John Hocking. These meetings made a great impression on our childhood, and amongst them we can remember the large temperance tea-parties our father gave in the Town Hall year by year at Easter. We sat amongst the people, and were allowed a cup of tea and a piece of plum cake like the others, afterwards taking our places behind father on the platform.

(Richard Cadbury of Birmingham)

All of the children were taught the importance of good manners, politeness and not exaggerating, and they were urged to be kind and respectful towards those employed by their parents. Above all, they were brought up as devout Quakers.

Despite living very close to their grandfather, a visit with Richard Tapper and Elizabeth Cadbury was a treat to look forward to. Nevertheless, their mother always ensured that they were turned out at their absolute best. Every week, on sixth days (Fridays), all of the grandchildren dined with Richard T. and Elizabeth. And on fourth days (Wednesdays), the entire family would attend a mid-week morning meeting at the Friends' Meeting House on Bull Street in Birmingham. The children also attended monthly and quarterly meetings, and quarterly meetings meant a half-day holiday from lessons.

Candia Barrow Cadbury spent the last twenty years of her life devoted to the total abstinence cause and she often called at homes where alcohol was generally a source of problems. She would even visit public houses in the roughest parts of Birmingham in her crusade. She died in March 1855 of consumption, probably contracted during one of her many home visits to the poorer people of Birmingham, and her widowed husband John would never fully recover from her death. It was their inheritance from their mother that George and Richard ploughed into their father's ailing chocolate business, although Richard also had the added responsibility of a new wife.

Richard's brother John, who only a few years earlier had been sent to Herefordshire both for the sake of his health and to learn farming, left his farm in England and made the long journey to a new life in Australia.

He had only been there twelve months or so by the spring of 1866 when Edward Cadbury, the youngest brother, died after a short illness. Edward was 22. News of his brother's death reached John in Australia, and merely a few weeks later he too was struck down by a sudden and fatal attack of what was called colonial fever. On 5 May, only three weeks earlier, John had written what was to be his last letter home:

> *It was pleasing to receive further intelligence of the last days of dear Edward, confirmatory to my faith that he gently sleeps in Jesus, and that rest with Him will indeed be but a moment, until the innumerable host are called to sing for ever with the harps of God.*

John Cadbury Sr lived to a grand age, despite suffering from melancholy since his wife's death and arthritis. He died in May 1889, aged 87.

Chapter 3

The world of work and adventure

Richard Cadbury initially started working at the Bridge Street factory as soon as he left school. Most sources say that this event occurred in 1850, but his daughter's biography of him, *Richard Cadbury of Birmingham*, says that it was the summer of 1851. Whilst it is possible he may have worked at the factory in the school holidays, he was still only 15 when he officially joined the firm. His Uncle Benjamin was still very much involved with the business and it was he and Richard's father John who were the original Cadbury brothers. In November 1853, the firm of Cadbury received royal appointment as cocoa and chocolate manufacturers to Queen Victoria.

Richard still enjoyed travelling and in the summer of 1854, he visited Switzerland with his friends Arthur Naish, the Reverend J.J. Brown, and a Mr Scott. He also enjoyed sport and exercise, playing football and climbing mountains whenever he had the chance. He played cricket and hockey and went sailing and skating. He even played for the firm's cricket team, which he started with his brother. During one match alone they are recorded as taking eleven wickets between them.

One employee, Henry Brewin, was to remember:

> It was customary [...] for cricket to take a prominent part, and we used to play in Sturge's field, near Wheeley's Road. I remember one match in particular, when it came to my turn to take the bat, the late Mr. Richard Cadbury being the bowler. He was very fond of the game, and could bowl a very swift ball.
>
> (*A History of Cadbury*)

Towards the end of 1854, Richard's brother John became unwell. He was still working at the shop in Bull Street, along with his cousin,

Richard Cadbury Barrow, but indoor life did not suit him and he collapsed twice, falling into a complete faint each time. Following the second episode, their father sent him to Herefordshire to learn farming and to live in the open air.

At around the time that Richard left school and went to work, his sister Maria was sent away to boarding school for two and a half years. She boarded with Mary, Myriam and Josephine Dymond in Lewes. When she was nearly 17 years old, at Christmas 1854, Maria left school and came home. Candia's health was failing and Maria's return was a great help to the ageing woman. However, Maria had only been at home for a few short months when Candia Barrow Cadbury died just one month short of her fiftieth birthday. Helen wrote:

> *She had only been at home for a month or two when sorrow fell like a crushing blow, leaving a blank in the lives of husband and children, which nothing could ever quite fill; for in March, 1855, the mother passed into the presence of the Saviour, whom she had loved and served so faithfully. It was one of the greatest griefs of Richard's life, for she had been so much to him – a friend and companion, as well as mother. In his boyhood they had spent many a happy hour studying botany together, and it was chiefly from her that he gained his love and knowledge of ferns and plants.*
>
> *(Richard Cadbury of Birmingham)*

Candia Barrow Cadbury was a kind woman who wanted nothing more than to help the poorer people of her time. One of her last acts was to visit a number of public houses where she spoke to the patrons and handed out pamphlets. Whether these people could read the pamphlets was, of course, another matter. One man remembered her kindness and wrote to George Cadbury fifty years after Candia's death:

> *In my youth I have worn clothing that your brothers John and Richard and yourself had left off, your dear mother taking care to clothe me, a poor orphan lad. To this day I can see her smile, and her gentle hands wrapping up parcels for me, and still hear her speaking to me words of kindness.*
>
> *(Richard Cadbury of Birmingham)*

At the time of her death, John Cadbury became seriously ill. He had rheumatic fever and suffered on and off for the rest of his life. He often had to go away for hydrotherapy (called hydropathy at the time), and could be gone for long periods at a time. The Victorians were very big on this cold water cure, which was used for all manner of ailments. Maria, although still very young, remained at home to care for her father until the day he died. Richard bore the brunt of his father's absence at work, although his Uncle Benjamin was still on hand to help and advise where he could. His brother George had finished school, but was in York learning about the tea trade.

The following year, in August 1856, Richard spent his twenty-first birthday alone. His brother John was at the farm in Herefordshire, brothers Edward and Henry were at school in Nottingham, and his father was at Southport, taking the waters with brother George and sister Maria. They all still remembered him though, and a bundle of letters arrived on the morning of his birthday. Some of the letters give some insight into how Richard intended on celebrating this special occasion. It was also his cousin Sarah's birthday at around the same time, and the family left in Birmingham had planned an excursion for the two young people.

John Jr wrote, from Stoke Hill:

DEAR BROTHER, – Thy letter, with details of various intended preparations to celebrate both thine and Cousin Sarah's birthday, is most truly interesting. Much as I should like to join you, I think I must defer my visit till father returns, or otherwise I should most certainly have come to Birmingham over-night to join your party. I hope this may reach you on the right and proper day, when with the usual compliments to thee, let me include Cousin Sarah, and wish you both many glad returns and a long and happy life. [...]

Maria wrote, from Southport:

MY OWN DEAR BROTHER, – Although we are all absent from thee, not for one moment think thou art forgotten by any of us, especially on so memorable a day as to-morrow, thy twenty-first birthday. It is a great pleasure to us to think that part of the day is to be spent at grandfather's. We have talked

21

*and thought of you much to-day, and hope you will all enjoy
the excursion, and that the day will be clear and fine; the
view then I should think would be extensive from the summit
of the Wrekin. Had George and I been at home, how we
should have enjoyed to join the party! Thou wilt be pleased
to hear that dear father really does seem to be benefiting
under the water cure, and at times is so lively and cheerful.*

John Sr wrote, from Southport:

*MY DEAR RICHARD, – This is intended to meet thee on the
29th of the present month, being thy twenty-first birthday,
an interesting and eventful period to all who are permitted
to attain to it; and in reviewing the course and events of thy
life, from they birth to the present time, it affords me the
truest pleasure and comfort to contemplate thy uniform
virtuous and amiable conduct. It is difficult to express all the
feelings of the mind on such an occasion as this, but I can
assure thee we are all most anxious to convey to thee the
near interest we feel on thy account, and we should like thy
twenty-first birthday to be one of great enjoyment to thee.
I much approve of thy proposal to have a day's excursion
with thy cousins in commemoration of it, and I wish it to
be carried out in a generous and liberal way, and of course
wholly at my expense. I am sorry I have been unable to
present thee with some useful and valuable memento of my
affection on thy birthday. It is my wish for thee to possess a
cabinet, suitable to contain thy specimens of butterflies and
other objects in which thou takes an interest. I wish thee to
order one according to thy own taste; I wish it to be good
and handsome.*

And then his father went on to drop the bombshell of his wish for Richard
to not only take more responsibility at the firm, but also to gradually take
over as head of the family. The letter continues:

*And now, dear Richard, in contemplating the present with
the future, I see the important and increasingly responsible*

position thou must necessarily hold in the business as well as in the family. I believe thou art not insensible to both, but as my own restoration to health is uncertain, I wish to encourage thee quietly and steadily to place thyself in my position, so as to be able with confidence to assume the important standing of a master. It is important for thee at all times to appear respectably dressed. I will not say more on this point, but conclude with the earnest and serious hope that neither business nor pleasure, or any other lawful pursuit, may interfere with the performance of thy civil and religious duties, so that the day's work may truly be said to keep pace with the day. Thou hast my entire confidence, and thou knows thou possesses the warmest love and affection of thy tenderly attached father.

Richard's Aunt Ann and his brother George also wrote letters from Southport, as did Henry and Edward from Nottingham.

Richard was joined at the works by his brother George in 1856, but in the summer of 1857 he had to turn down the offer of a holiday in Dartmoor from his old schoolfriend C.W. Dymond. Their father had taken ill again and was away from home and Richard had to hold down the fort at work. Almost as if to rub salt in, his friend wrote to him on 8 August 1857:

DEAR RICHARD, – I was very sorry that thou wast under the necessity of giving up going with us to Dartmoor. We took five days for a ramble round the borders and through the centre on the moor. [...] Many of the views we obtained were remarkably fine, and some of the scenery of the interior of the moor wild and solitary in the extreme. [...] I often wished thou had been with us, for thou would have enjoyed it so much. It is very pleasing to hear that John has now got a farm of his own. He will no doubt do well, as he seems to take great interest in farming. It will be a very pleasant place for you to visit now and then during the summer.

Thy affectionate friend,
C.W. DYMOND.

The previous year, in September 1856, plans had been started to buy brother John his farm.

John Cadbury seems to have been well aware of the extra responsibility placed upon his son's shoulders, for when Richard was about 23, his father ensured he had some time off. Richard made his third trip to Switzerland on this occasion. Helen wrote:

> [...] *His father had again been very ill, and was at Southport with Maria.*
>
> *Richard had been steadily working away at Bridge Street, and his father felt he had well earned another trip abroad.* [...] *Many remember the stories of terrible climbs and exciting adventures, and Richard wrote a descriptive diary for his father, profusely illustrated with sketches made from rough drawings on the spot, and coloured and finished at home. One of his climbs which he made with his guide, who became his devoted friend and admirer, was the Col de Géant, and was one of the earliest ascents of this mountain. One of his sketches represents a precipitous rock, up which he and the guide, roped together, were cautiously and laboriously climbing, cutting steps as they went. On the summit of the rock stood a young chamois, looking down on them.* [...] *Other pictures show them roped, and crossing snowfields or cutting their way along ledges of ice. There is one of the Hospice of St. Bernard, with an account of the visit to that place, telling of the little garden where the monks tried to grow some cabbages, and succeeded in getting one about the size of a walnut. A rather ghastly sketch shows the Mortuary, with the dim outlines of silent figures lying within, where those who had lost their friends on the mountains went to try and recognise them among these frozen and disfigured remains.*
>
> (*Richard Cadbury of Birmingham*)

Richard Cadbury was still a young man and he had a lot of responsibility on his shoulders, but he was determined to enjoy life to the full. He belonged to a circle of Friends who enjoyed country pursuits, nature, the outdoors, and excursions in general. The walks he enjoyed before breakfast on his own or with just one companion when he was at school were now a fixture of his business life, except now he was accompanied by a group of fellow walkers. Because they were all employed, they still had to fit their walks in before breakfast, and they would take it in turns meeting at each other's houses, a different house each time. It was so early when these fellows met up at the designated home that the rest of the household was still fast asleep.

Provisions were left out for the ramblers and they would cook bacon, sausages and toast and drink coffee before setting off on their walks. Even on dark winter mornings they would still gather, and the ice and frost brought with it yet more activity, particularly skating. Richard was one of the finest ice skaters his friends and acquaintances knew. His brother George recalled many of his favourite pastimes:

> *He was passionately fond of skating, and, when a young man, frequently rose at five o'clock so as to be on the ice before the dawn of day, and thus have two hours' exercise before going to business in the city. Only those who have made this effort know the exhilaration of skating in the early morning, and watching the light gradually break and the beauty of the sunrise. He was fond of athletic exercises, and was always captain of the football and hockey team that played at Edgbaston [...] being an exceptionally good player at both games. [...] In later years he often longed, amid the pressure of business, for more time in which to engage in the exercises and games of his youth and early manhood.*
>
> (*Richard Cadbury of Birmingham*)

Richard and his chums could often be found skating in the winter on Edgbaston Reservoir, which was built in 1827 by Thomas Telford. Originally called Roach Pool, and found within Rotton Park, the lake was fed by a number of small streams. The valley was dammed, by Telford, and the reservoir extended twice between then and when Richard Cadbury and his friends were skating there. Local legend says that, later, J.R.R. Tolkien based his famous 'two towers of Gondor' on two landmarks that can still be seen at Edgbaston Reservoir today. However, only one was standing at the time of Richard's youthful visits.

Perrott's Folly was built in 1758 by John Perrott, who owned the land at the time, apparently so he could spy on his errant wife. It is said that the folly was the inspiration for Tolkien's Minas Tirith. The other tower is the Victorian pumping station, or Edgbaston Waterworks, which is said to have been the inspiration for Minas Morgul. That wasn't built until 1870, which was still in Richard's lifetime, but it would not have been there when he and his friends were causing mayhem. Of course, other towers around the country also claim to be Tolkein's muses, but as Birmingham also has the Sandyman Mill (Sarehole Mill in Hall Green), the locals like to cling to their beliefs.

Edgbaston Reservoir is still there today, although the surroundings have become much more built-up in the intervening years. It's a popular birdwatching location, and there is a pretty walk around the perimeter that still gives a flavour of how it might have looked more than 150 years ago.

One of Richard's ice skating friends recalled on amusing incident that happened elsewhere in Edgbaston. Helen recounted the tale in her biography of her father, *Richard Cadbury of Birmingham*:

> [...] *Samuel Price* [was] *one of the skating fraternity. Although the reservoir at Edgbaston was the place where they most often enjoyed their favourite recreation, the large pool at the foot of the Edgbaston Hall grounds offered temptations which could not be resisted. One winter there was an exceptionally long hard frost, and during part of the time the moon was full. With the frosty ground crunching beneath their feet, the young fellows made their way to the borders of Edgbaston Park; they climbed over the palings, taking care not to break or injure them, and were soon skimming over the frozen pool in the moonlight. Their surreptitious visits continued, and as they grew bolder they used to go in the early mornings as well. Sometimes when it was dark they burned coloured fires on the ice. This led to the detection of their pranks, and old Lawyer Whateley, who lived at the Hall, set to work to put a stop to them. One morning he sent a man down to the pool to take the young men's names, and to request them not to come again.* [It] *happened that Lawyer Whateley was a friend of that*

*stately and dignified old Quaker, Richard's grandfather.
The similarity of the names at once struck Mr. Whateley. He
well knew, of course, that it was a young man who had been
skating; but he wrote a letter to Richard Tapper Cadbury,
who was nearly ninety at this time, saying he was sorry that
his old friend had taken the trouble to* climb over his palings
to skate, *as he would have been glad to let him in by the
gate at any time. The idea of the old gentleman climbing
over the palings was very amusing, and evidently half in
fun; but Richard Tapper Cadbury took it quite seriously,
and wrote to say how surprised he was that his friend, John
Welshman Whateley, should think him capable of such a
piece of ill-manners. Needless to say, this was the end of
stolen visits to Edgbaston pool, for Richard's grandfather,
though not without a keen sense of humour and sincere love
for his grandchildren, was a strict disciplinarian, and had a
great sense of the proprieties.*

The current Edgbaston Hall was built in 1717 after the original medieval manor house, which was mentioned in the *Domesday Book*, was burnt down at the end of the English Civil War. The gardens were designed by Lancelot "Capability" Brown in 1776. A listed grade II building, the hall stands in an elevated position with panoramic views to the south of the city and was leased out from 1783 for the next 150 years. In 1936, Edgbaston Golf Club took over the lease and the park was laid out as a golf course, but the hall was requisitioned by the War Office during the Second World War.

Later that same winter, Samuel Price was skating with his friend on Edgbaston Reservoir when he inadvertently skated onto a particularly thin part of the ice that subsequently collapsed beneath his weight. It was only Richard's fast thinking that saved him. Seeing what had happened, Richard skated towards his friend straight away, calling the others to follow him and knotting two handkerchiefs together as he went. Richard lay flat on the ice, telling the next to arrive at the spot to do the same and grab hold of his heels as he inched towards the break in the ice. Samuel grabbed hold of the knotted hankies and he was pulled to safety. It was so cold that by the time they reached his home, running all the way, Samuel's clothes were board-stiff.

During his youth, J.W. Shorthouse was one of Richard's best friends. Shorthouse wrote:

As a boy he was strong and a very fast runner, and many pleasant games at cricket and hockey I have had in his company in Joseph Sturge's field. We sometimes had great fun at his father's house in Calthorpe Road, especially on one occasion, when we had a bonfire and fireworks there, attended by Friends generally. He also went with us on boating expeditions, notably in the year 1858, when we arranged one on the Wye from its mouth to Hay. His brother John was then farming in Herefordshire. The best sketches illustrating the account of this expedition were done by Richard Cadbury, who had much artistic taste. As a boy and a young man he had the same characteristics as in later life, great determination to take his full share of any work that had to be done, and a desire to make things pleasant for all who were working or playing with him. I should not think he ever said an unkind word to any one. [...] We all felt we got in him a better man than ourselves, and he was so good-natured that he seldom declined.

(Richard Cadbury of Birmingham)

Charles Lean, a fellow Friend, remembered:

We never met without the cheery "Well, Charles," and kind inquiries. [...] I chiefly remember our games, and always envied his bold wheeling round the gymnastic pole. We and others enjoyed together in their season cricket, football, skating, bathing, bonfires, and fireworks at his father's. We attended debates at the Friends' Reading Society and a Bible Class at Bull Street. In all he was thorough and determined, and a good example to any one.

(Richard Cadbury of Birmingham)

In the spring of 1859, the Society of Friends mourned the passing of that wonderful man who brought adult education to Birmingham and who let young men play games in his field: Joseph Sturge. And the following year, on 13 March, Richard's grandfather, Richard Tapper Cadbury, died.

In the summer of 1860, a contingent from the American side of the family came over for a tour of Europe. The four cousins stopped off in Birmingham on the way and attended a big family party thrown in their honour at Richard Tapper Cadbury's house. A few weeks later, Richard Barrow Cadbury joined them on the rest of their tour, along with an uncle from Banbury and another cousin.

There follow a number of letters describing this tour that Richard Barrow Cadbury wrote home, reproduced here as an accurate account in his own words, to give a flavour of what it would have been like. The letters are quite vivid and serve as wonderful written illustrations from a time when cameras were not a common household item:

HÔTEL DE LILLE ET D'ALBION, PARIS.
September 13th, 1860.
DEAR FATHER, – I have just received thy letter, which arrived about mid-day. We had a splendid passage over from Folkestone, with scarcely a cloud on the sky, and the scene as we left the white cliffs of Albion [poetic Dover] *was indeed very beautiful. The sea was quite an emerald green colour, and the atmosphere so clear that we could distinctly see the small crescent of the moon and Venus, a brilliant object a little to the right, although the sun was shining brightly. We saw also many seagulls, some of which came close to the bows of the vessel. On our arrival at Boulogne we saw as usual some of the universal French soldiers, with their red peg-top trousers, their hands as if fastened in their pockets. We got our luggage through the Douane without much trouble, and put up at the Hôtel de Paris, as we were just too late to get off by the 10.30 train. We then strolled about the town, and saw its beautiful cathedral, with some rather extraordinary crypts underneath, covered with rough paintings, this part being all that remained of the old cathedral which was battered down with cannon. We had some capital fun. Uncle James found many that could speak some English, but it did not much matter whether or no – he gave it them, and some curious scenes we had*

between signs and words until we undertook to help him out. We left by a train at 5.30, and arrived in Paris at 11.0 [sic] *after a very pleasant ride, and with plenty to keep us merry. We are very comfortably located here, John Warder, Joel, and I in one room, and Caroline, Sarah, and Martha Gibbins in a most elegantly furnished apartment, where we are now all writing our letters.* [There is no mention of how Uncle James was accommodated.] *We have had a very busy day; Uncle James and myself got up at half-past five to explore the district, and walked through the gardens of the Tuileries, in which the flowers were most luxuriant – long beds covered by one mass of plants and scarcely one that was not in flower; among the trees further on were quite a forest of chairs, where the people congregate in the evenings. We then passed on to the Place de la Concorde, and had a peep through a telescope at the planet Venus, showing it about the size of the moon, and not more than one-half lit by the sun, thus* [there follows an illustration of a crescent moon waxing]. *We went on to the fruit-market, two or three times the size of Covent Garden, and quantities of the most delicious fruit; we bought about 120 greengages, which have been most acceptable during the day.*

We met the rest of the party at breakfast at nine o'clock, as we thought they ought to have a good night, and started at ten, the first part being what uncle and I had seen before breakfast, with the exception of the fruit-market. The Louvre really cannot be described with justice. From the immense courtyard enclosed within it we could look with amazement upon the magnificent range of architectural beauty around us. The high buildings of which it is composed seem an elaborate display of columns, statues, and carved stone work. We made our entrance into the museum, and were soon lost amongst paintings of the very highest order, and think we did not walk less than a mile in viewing them – Raphaels, Caraccis, Murillos, and thousands of others. We really could hardly tell how to leave, they were so enchanting; we had no time to see the sculptures. At about three we went into a small restaurant, and had a good dinner for a franc each, sitting in a kind of trellised balcony, covered with creepers. We gave the waiter sundry commands in French and English, Uncle James at last giving in with the latter. I don't know what folks will think of us, for we laugh so much. After this we went to the Hôtel de Ville, and were taken over all the state apartments – Napoleon's reception-room, and the splendid ballroom where he gave that ball that we read of some time ago in the papers. From thence to the Cathedral of Notre Dame; the carved stone-work in front was particularly curious and beautiful. We then walked to the column of Juliet, where we all got into a diligence and went for three or four miles along the principal boulevards of Paris to the Madeleine; this we found was just closed, but we shall see it to-morrow if we have time. After some tea at our hotel and some writing, we have just been all along the Champs-Elysées and Place de la Concorde by gaslight – a very fine sight, with thousands of lights making it quite a fairy scene; we then went for a mile and a half along some of the finest boulevards, to see the cafés and restaurants and shops of all kinds, dressed out with a taste such as only Parisians can show. Excuse so rough and poor an epitome of what we have been witnessing, but it is impossible in so short a time to do justice to it. Cousins wish to join me in dear love to thee and all at home, and I remain,

Thy affectionate son,
R. CADBURY.

MAÇON, September 15th, 1860.
MY DEAR FATHER, – We arrived here this morning at 4.30, after a comfortable ride from Paris; Uncle James and I did not take beds, as we thought we had had enough sleep, but have enjoyed a bath and a walk around the town. The River Saone is wide here, but its banks are flat and uninteresting. We bought two bunches of grapes, quite ½ lb. each, for 2d. (4 sous), which were delicious. Yesterday we made our way at ten o'clock to the Jardin des Plantes, which disappointed us very much; certainly nothing to compare with our Zoological Gardens, either in

plants or animals. We took a cab from here to the Pantheon, from the top of which we had a splendid panoramic view of Paris, and it was interesting to consult our map, to trace all the public buildings and gardens. The beautiful gardens of the Luxembourg were close to us, and here we walked to next. The arrangement of trees, flowers, and marble statues is much finer than anything I have ever seen before. The pictures in the palace are mostly by French artists; several amongst them of Rosa Bonheur's best paintings. We were much surprised here, as in the Louvre, to notice so many artists copying the pictures, and one-half of these ladies; but the latter were not so much masters of the brush as the former, excepting in miniatures. By this time we were somewhat hungry, and made a descent upon a pâtissier's, which was a salutary change, and then turned our steps to the Hôtel Cluny, and ancient palace, the rooms of which were decorated with a very remarkable collection of antiquities. There were some of the best productions of Palissy, the potter, and the most beautiful tapestry I ever saw, quite equal to a good painting. There were a great quantity of exquisite carvings in wood and ivory, and curiosities of all kinds, mostly connected with the kings of France. This was to me the most interesting of anything that we have seen in Paris, and was a good finish to the day's sight-seeing. We returned to our hotel in time for a table d'hôte at half-past five; and this was quite a novelty to cousins, being the first we have yet had, and they were thoroughly tired out before we got through it. Uncle James amuses us very much, in asking for potatoes with his beef, and stale bread instead of new, clean plates after cheese for dessert, etc.; but we are all settling down to thorough French life, and he enjoys it as much as any of us. He went with me both mornings in Paris about six o'clock to wander through the streets, which were thronged with people, and to the markets, where we regaled ourselves upon pears, peaches, and greengages; we bought eight splendid peaches for 1s., which we took home for breakfast with the others. We also saw the Billingsgate of Paris, with exactly the same scene as in London, only that the clamour was in a foreign tongue, and they employ women who sit on high desks to take account of what is sold, and receive the money. I think we certainly had far the best of it, for the mornings were so fresh and cool, and the people more astir than in the middle of the day. It has begun to rain a little this morning, but think it will clear up. We shall spend a quiet day in Geneva to-morrow, reaching there about ten this evening. Since writing the above, uncle and I have been out again, and crossed to the other side of the river, where there is a large fair; and as there is a little rain all the people have umbrellas up, forming quite a curious scene, as they are all colours, a quarter of them bright scarlet. They were selling quantities of pears and apples in long sacks, grapes, peaches, nectarines, and one part of it was a sort of corn-market – sacks of all kinds ranged in long rows with the sellers at the back – doubtless for the small farmers which this country abounds in. The carts are all drawn by bullocks and cows, and form an interesting sight wending their way to market. The women almost all wear the curious chimney hat with broad flat brim.

I must now close this, as we are going to have dinner, and then on to the station for Geneva. Farewell, with dear love,

Thine very affectionately,
R. CADBURY.

CHAMOUNIX, September 18th, 1860.
DEAR FATHER, – We are boxed in here this afternoon by some rain, and we are therefore spending a few hours in writing home. We received thy acceptable letters, and also one from Cousin Elizabeth, to whom please give my dear love and thanks. It is very interesting to me to go over ground that I have been over before, and I think that its beauties are doubly fixed upon the memory, and far more appreciated for doing so. From Mâcon to Geneva we passed by the railroad through the magnificent valley at one end of the Jura range, often with precipitous rocks on one side,

and a beautiful sloping mountain on the other, laid out in cornfields and vineyards. We spent the next day (First Day) very enjoyably at Geneva. Cousins Sarah, Martha, and I went to the English church, and had a very practical sermon preached us; the others stayed at the hotel and sat together for a time of quiet devotion. When we returned we all set out for a walk, and visited the cemetery, which is prettily laid out. Calvin's tomb is simply a small stone, with the initials marked upon it at the foot of the grave. This was his particular wish, that no tombstone should be raised over his grave. We also saw the tomb of Sir H. Davey, and some few other notables. We then followed the beautifully blue and clear Rhône to its junction with the Arve; there is a little promontory that runs out for some way between the rivers, and so narrow that you can place your hands at the same time in both. The Arve was very much swollen, as was the Rhône, by the quantities of rain that had fallen upon the mountains, and a gentleman told us that the Rhône was two feet higher than the day before; the junction of the muddy waters of the Arve with the clear ones of the Rhône was very curious. In the evening, after a table d'hôte at five, we went to the poste restante *for your letters, which only opens at 6 p.m. on a First Day, and very much enjoyed reading some of them together aloud; after which we had another stroll by starlight through the town, and on to a new pier or breakwater, that they have built opposite to the town. We ordered for the morning a carriage with three horses for Chamounix, and we were all ready for them at seven o'clock. The country through which we passed it is very difficult to describe; we were all exceedingly charmed by its beauty and grandeur – the little Swiss* châlets *dotted about among corn fields and meadows, which extended for some miles, and backed by some grand rocky peak towering up among the fleecy clouds that clung to it. The quantity of fruit-trees and fruit was really something wonderful – plums of six or seven descriptions, apples and pears, and all of them open to any one who likes to take them; for instance, we would drive our carriage under a plum-tree, and then; taking hold of the stem, shake a deluge of them upon us; we really got so many that we did not know what to do with them, and I am sure I never ate more in my life at one time. Some of them were particularly delicious, and we did so wish we could import some of them over to you. The latter part of the way was amongst pine-forests and very steep, so that we had to walk a great part of the way. Joel and I walked the last nine miles, and enjoyed it extremely, and as each snowy peak came into view, ribbed with its glaciers, every step seemed to add to the magnificence of the scene. The Glacier des Boissons seemed as if it poured its white frozen torrent in our path, and was a beautiful object. We are stopping at the same hotel (La Couronne) that George and Richard C. Barrow stopped at, and find it very comfortable. This morning we procured four mules and three guides, and were all ready by eight o'clock, not at all discouraged by the rain which had fallen through a great part of the night. We made quite a remarkable appearance, uncle, John Warder, Joel, and I having on our light coats strapped round the waist and trousers tucked into our boots; cousins were all wrapped up well in shawls, and we all felt in splendid spirits. It took us two hours to arrive at the Montauvert, and as it cleared up and the sun shone brightly before we got half-way, the views down in the valley below us and the mountains on the other side were beautiful. We made arrangements with the guides to have our mules taken to the other side of the glacier, so that we might cross it, and have them ready for us. This we easily accomplished, and all much enjoyed it, and it gave us a fair idea of what glaciers really are. The view from the Château, where the ice breaks up, is very fine, showing the exquisite blue colour that is the great charm of glacier ice. We intend going up the Flégère to-morrow if nothing prevents us in reference to weather, etc. I hope to write you again from Interlaken, or perhaps before this. There has been a great deal of talking, and I am afraid this is much disconnected. With dear love to all, I remain,*

Thy affectionate son,
R. CADBURY.

It is interesting to see that the men wore 'light coats' and the ladies wore 'shawls', which can't have been much protection against the elements in such a cool climate. They would also have been wearing ordinary, everyday shoes or boots.

THUN, September 23rd, 1860.

DEAR FATHER, – I believe that my last letter was posted at Chamounix, since which time we have been through a great deal of the most charming Alpine scenery. Last Fourth Day was very wet and heavy, clouds hanging on the mountains, so we decided instead of ascending the Flégère to go straight off to Martigny; we got five mules, one of which was for the luggage, and commenced our day's journey, as the one before, in soaking rain. It soon, however, cleared up, and we had a favourable day. We stopped for dinner at a little hotel, facing the beautiful fall of the Barbarme, which dashes down the mountain and sends the spray on all sides. The single path runs most of the way on the side of the mountain, and the peeps into the deep valley with the river foaming below were very fine; it is, however, finest near the summit of the Téte Noire, where the valley widens and deepens, and the river finds a channel down the valley and gorge of the Trient into that of the Rhône. At the summit of the Forclay we had to have our tickets viséed for the Vallais; it seemed a curious thing to be stopped there, almost on the verge of the eternal snow. The last five or six miles cousins joined us on foot, being thoroughly tired of riding, and the guides took us by a short cut through fields and orchards, and I should think we had such a run as they never had before; but really the mountain air gives you such life and strength that you become almost like the chamois. We slept that night at Martigny, and hired a large carriage to take us to Leukerbad in the morning. It was rather a dry ride the first part, along the valley of the Rhône; but directly we turned into the valley of Leuk the scenery was most magnificent. As cousins say, each day the views are grander than the former. This was the valley that Arthur Naish and I walked down at midnight on our last tour together, and it was very interesting to see in reality what I had only conjectured at before. Some of the little villages situated on the sloping sides of the mountains, and half hidden in orchards, and the white steeple of its little church, formed a picturesque scene, and just as evening's twilight crept over the landscape, they rung a peal of fine bells, completing the enchantment. Leukerbad itself is situated at the very end of the valley, and is quite hemmed in by precipitous rocks. Over these is the pass of the Gemmi, and it being a splendid morning (Sixth Day) we got the necessary mules and guides and set off at eight o'clock. The path is so narrow, and winds so much among the cliffs, that no part of it can be seen from the bottom. We found it very steep, but it was more difficult in proportion for the ladies on mules than for us; but all labour was amply repaid as the distant scenery gradually extended and everything below us appeared in miniature. There had been a great deal of snow the night before, and the last half-mile the ground was covered with it, and on the summit above, 7,000 feet high, the snow was some four or five inches deep. We could see from here most of the snowy peaks of the Monte Rosa Range – the Matterhorn, Weisshorn, etc. – reminding me of my late trip amongst their snows and valleys. The descent of the pass was extremely beautiful, and grander than any we have passed, as we had snowy mountains on each side of us. We picked some of the holly fern, just where I obtained that which is growing in our rockery, to bring home with us for Cousin Martha. The mules went with us as far as Kandersteg, where we got return carriages to Interlaken. The scenery was thoroughly Swiss. The people seem to take great pride in their cottages – almost all of them with the woodwork carved, and in some cases quite elaborately. We took up our quarters at a capital hotel, the Belvedere in Interlaken, and as we had missed one day at Chamounix we determined to make up for it here, so I arranged for carriages and mules to take us in the morning over the Wengernalp, We drove as far as Lauterbrunnen, and sent the carriages to meet us at Grindelwald, while we made the tour of the Wengernalp to that place. My ideas in connection with Lauterbrunen were very pleasant ones, and I was not at all disappointed, as it lies amongst the most beautiful valleys. The peasant girls also wear a very pretty dress, one of which I was tempted to buy, and will bring home with me. About a quarter of a mile from here is the Staubbach (or Dust Fall), the most beautiful waterfall I have seen in Switzerland. It falls over a projecting ledge of rock 950 feet above the valley, and it is impossible to describe with justice the beauty of the feathery arrows of water that shoot from the summit, gradually dispersing themselves, till they all fall in a misty cloud to the bottom. On each side of the main fall was a slender stream of water that seemed as if hung in mid-air, for its tiny current was almost all dissolved into mist before reaching the bottom; but the finishing touch was an exquisite rainbow at the bottom of the main fall, extending in a right angle from the rock, the colours being as vivid as I ever remember seeing in a rainbow. We were quite sorry to leave the scene, but we had a long day's work before us, and could not stop longer. The ascent of the pass is at first very steep, and a tremendous pull it was; but we seem always repaid for hard work, and so it was here in the view spread out before us. The echoes among the rocks are particularly grand in these mountains. In two or three places on our route people were stationed, who lived in some of the little châlets *and blew a large Alpine horn, I should think six feet long, which resounded from hill to hill, sometimes in its reverberations equalling the notes of an organ. The most magnificent scene was in store for us at the summit, as we faced nearly the whole range of the Oberland. The Great and Small Giant, the Jung-Frau, Silberhorn, and other snowy mountains were all at our feet; their glaciers and snowfields seemed quite close to us. This is also the best place to see avalanches, of which we saw at least eight or ten while we were there. It is quite awe-inspiring to hear the distant thunder of the masses of ice as they break off from the side of the glacier, and are at once dashed into powder among the rocks; and here you may judge of real distance, as all you can see is a small dusty cloud rushing down the mountain side. I have not time to describe more, excepting to say that we had a delightful ride back to Interlaken, well satisfied with our day's work. We went some of us to the English chapel to service in the morning (First Day), and had a stroll to the Lake of Brientz; in the afternoon we took the steamer on the Lake of Thun to Thun – a most delightful and memorable farewell it was to the Alps, as we watched the shadows gradually steal up their snowy sides, which were tinged with the most lovely pink or roseate hue; and when the last rays had left the highest peak, the atmosphere above them partook of the same pinky colour, throwing out in bold relief the snowy mountains, which now appeared of the purest whiteness. In a few minutes the moon with the planet Mars shone with a silvery light in the heavens, and were reflected in the mirrored waters of the lake, which shone like polished steel. Farewell for the present, with dear love,*

> *Thy affectionate son,*
> *R. CADBURY.*

With such a vivid pen picture, who needs photographs?

On 27 September, Richard wrote a few lines from Folkestone to his father to let him know that they would be home the following evening. They had enjoyed a comfortable journey across the Channel for their third night but the previous two days had been rough at sea. On their return they were invited to Brighton and decided to spend the last evening of their journey there.

Chapter 4

The firm of Cadbury

Much of the history of the Cadbury manufactory is covered in *A History of Cadbury* by this same author. However, as the company featured so heavily in Richard Cadbury's life, here is an overview.

The firm of Cadbury had already moved from the Crooked Lane site to a new premises in Bridge Street, via a brief period in Cambridge Street, by the time Richard joined the company in 1850/51. It is possible he may have worked at the factory in the school holidays but he was still only 15 when he officially joined the firm. He recalled that there was a store house, roasting ovens, a kibbling mill and various other machinery on the ground floor, and there was a light and airy packing room on the floor above.

Richard was followed by his brother George in 1856. Their father was still suffering the after effects of rheumatic fever and when their mother died, in 1855, John Cadbury also sank into a deep depression. The trade was already in a rapid decline, along with the quality of the product, and John Cadbury's failing health could not have helped matters. By 1859, there were only twenty-or-so workers at the Bridge Street factory.

Sources differ on the amount Richard and George inherited from their mother, from £4,000 each to £5,000 each to £10,000 and £12,000 between them. Whatever the amount, both sank as much as they could into turning the firm around, and Richard was apparently left with around £150, and he'd had a family to support at the same time. In 1914, George Cadbury wrote when remembering the struggle:

> *I was spending at that time for travelling, clothing, charities, and everything else about £25 a year. My brother had married, and at the end of five years he had only £150. If I had been married there would have been no Bournville*

to-day – it was just the money that I saved by living so
sparely that carried us over the crisis.

(Life of George Cadbury)

John Cadbury retired in 1861 and Richard and George took control
of the company. Richard was 25 and newly married, George was 21
(some sources say 22), and their first task was to save the company. For
three years both men lived without any indulgences and worked hard
until they got the firm back on its feet. They worked from 7.30 am until
8.00 pm, six days a week. In the first three years, the company made
serious losses and the brothers started to discuss what they might do if
they decided to wind down the firm, but in 1864, they finally recorded a
small profit. These early years were without doubt difficult, but the two
men followed *The Book of Christian Discipline of the Religious Society
of Friends*, which was a kind of work or self-help manual published
in 1883.

At the time the brothers took over, Mr T.J. O'Brien worked in the
crèmes department as a beater, beating the mixture for the fillings. He
remembered:

> *During these trying times I never knew men work harder
> than our masters who were indeed more like fathers to us.
> Sometimes they were working in the manufactory, then
> packing in the warehouse, then again all over the country
> getting orders.*

(Cadbury's Angels)

Not only was the firm in trouble during this period, it was also making
an inferior product, bulked out with additives probably in a bid to help
make ends meet as much as in ignorance. But the end consumer was
not content with this inferior product. In defence of the company, in a
speech in 1921, reported below, George Cadbury spoke of how the firm
was still a producer of mostly tea and coffee:

> *Cocoa formed only a very small part of the trade – about
> one fourth. In those days they used only as much cocoa in
> the year as is now used [1921] at Bournville in an hour.
> They made a cocoa of which they were not very proud ...*

only one fifth of it was cocoa, the rest being potato starch, sago, flour and treacle. Other manufacturers made the same article – a comforting gruel.

Among the thirty manufacturers engaged in the trade at that time they [the Cadburys] *were the smallest, and they made about the lowest class of goods. He* [George] *and his brother* [Richard] *always pulled together, but they had a very uphill fight. The small shopkeepers were constantly failing, and the firm lost money. They were not content, however, to go on making such extremely common cocoa, and after six years they made a cocoa for drinking, taking out the cocoa butter instead of adding flour to counteract it. They were the first firm in the Kingdom to do so.*

(The Firm of Cadbury: 1831 – 1931)

George and Richard's younger brother Henry joined the firm in 1869, working in the Bridge Street offices first before becoming a 'traveller'. Today he would probably be called a travelling salesman. By 1870, the workforce had reached 200 once again. But the brothers would never forget their early struggles.

'They never forgot how near they were to closing the business,' wrote Helen Cadbury Alexander in 1906. 'Often during these early struggles Richard Cadbury would say to his brother, "If I had a few hundreds a year for certain I should love to retire and enjoy the country." But when success came, both felt that it would be their duty, not only to those whom they employed, but to a far wider circle, to stick to their business, which Richard Cadbury did to the very end of his life.'

One of Richard's first jobs every day was to open the post. On 14 February 1871, a pile of valentine cards arrived at Bridge Street addressed to some of the women working there. Richard kept them in the office until the end of the working day as he didn't want any unnecessary excitement to distract the ladies from their work. Letters arrived at Bournville by a horse-drawn van, and often this van would pick Richard up on the way in as well. He called the letter van his chariot and would jump on board at Dogpool Lane, where he'd walked each morning from his home now in Moseley. Later, his sons would help him with this daily letter-opening task.

Mr G.W. Brice worked in the finance department, and he remembered the atmosphere in the office:

> *I was only a young stripling when I first entered the employ of Mr Richard and Mr George Cadbury which was in the midsummer of 1872.*
>
> *[...] Our office was one of serene quietness: apart from the noise created by the turning over of the leaves of a ledger and the replacing of a book in the rack, only the scratch of the pen could be heard. The letterbox was in the wall at the back of Mr Richard's desk; He used to open the letters – not a very large task in those days – and the orders were handed over to Mr Truman. We used the tab and card system, so after the orders were entered in day books and copied onto the tabs for packing, either Mr George or Mr Richard would come and sit between two of us, taking the original order while George Truman took the tab.*
>
> *(Cadbury's Angels)*

Another of his regular responsibilities was tasting the tea, along with his father, John Cadbury, and his cousin, Richard Cadbury Barrow. Tea tasting took place on a Saturday morning.

They did have their own quarters, though, and their office looked out upon a rose garden. During the summer months, the roses from this garden were sent to the grocery exchange in Manchester and on to the firm's customers.

Barrow Cadbury, Richard's eldest son, was to recall:

> *Father would often go into the warehouse and in the simplest way make up orders himself. This was of course necessary in the early days when the hands were few, but even in his later years he would enjoy a good busy afternoon helping in this way. His artistic taste was very useful in the business – many of the early pictures, before colour printing was so general, were of his own design, and the choosing of pictures for the fancy boxes was in his department. His office window, also Uncle George's, looked out on to a pleasant garden with rose beds and shrubs, a very great contrast to*

the dingy cramped little offices in Bridge Street. When they came to Bournville Father and Uncle realised that a large part of their lives would be spent in their offices and for this reason they thus arranged them. He [Richard] *arrived at the business at 8.25 daily. He was always approachable to any of his workpeople and they felt to have in him a personal friend. Father began work at the age of 15, and so in many ways he was self taught.*

[...] *No two partners ever worked in more complete harmony than the two Cadbury brothers, Richard and George ...*

There was a private passage between [their] *two offices, and consultations were taking place continually in one office or the other, and, as I had no other* pied a terre *at Bournville than my father's office, I was often present at these private conversations.*

(*Barrow Cadbury*)

Richard designed the illustrations for the chocolate boxes while George made his product-changing trip to Holland (see *A History of Cadbury* by Diane Wordsworth for more information). Richard was a natural salesman and became accomplished at credit control. Many of the firm's problems were also down to the customer as quite a few would often drag their feet over paying their bills. Each morning, Richard would go over any new orders and decide whether or not they should be honoured, or if perhaps part of the order may be supplied. This would depend on the individual customer's history with the company. And then there was the quality of the product, which is mentioned above.

George and Richard's brother Henry joined the firm in around 1869. But at the end of 1875, he had contracted typhoid fever and, sadly, died. It had been nine years since his brothers John and Edward had died, and Henry had only been married for two years. He also left behind an infant daughter. The workers had assembled for their usual morning prayers when they heard the sad news. The hymn they had planned on singing was called *Knocking, Knocking, Who is there?*, but most broke down before they were able to reach the end. When Richard tried to read from the Bible, he could not do it. He broke down, placed his head in his hands, and wept. George tried to do the reading instead, but by then the gathering was content to sit in quiet and tearful contemplation.

One of the forewomen said: 'We all felt we had lost an elder brother.' (*Richard Cadbury of Birmingham*) And Richard wrote in the family book: *During his latter years he often laid stress upon the power of the blood shed on Calvary to cleanse from the guilt of sin, not relying on any works of his own, but on the atoning Sacrifice.*

In 1878, building began on a new factory surrounded by countryside on the outskirts of Birmingham. Construction also started on sixteen semi-detached cottages that had gardens. These cottages were destined for the foremen and other senior workers. For those who would still be commuting from Birmingham town centre, cheaper rail fares were negotiated. What was known then as Stirchley Street Station became known as Bournville Station. Richard and George were almost constantly on the site overseeing the works, and their father was another regular visitor.

The first brick was laid in January 1879 and by July the old factory at Bridge Street was closed. In September, the brothers moved the factory from the centre of Birmingham to Bournville, and Richard was so excited by the move that he bought a batch of rail tickets for some of the girls and accompanied them on their first day at work at the new premises.

During the winter at the Bournville factory, Richard Cadbury would reveal his courteous side. There was no shelter at the railway station, so he would encourage the female workers to wait in their heated dressing room until the train was on its way. Then he would blow a whistle and the girls could run straight out to the train without hanging around in the cold. Fanny Price remembered this quite well:

In cold and rainy weather, shelter for the girls was provided near the old station lodge; Mr Richard used to stand outside and blow a whistle to intimate that the train was coming so that the girls could run from their dressing room. Several of the employees who were young at that time and not very well off, received free railway tickets through the kindness of one or other of their masters.

(*Cadbury's Angels*)

He could also often be seen about the factory helping the girls to lift boxes. Employee Tom Hackett remembered:

> *It was no unusual thing to see* [Mr. Richard] *carrying a pile of boxes from one of the Boxing Rooms in order to expedite the despatch* [sic] *of the Orders from the Warehouse. In doing this he would sometimes lay down his Cap (which he often carried in his hands when in the Works) and some while afterwards would come back to find it.*
>
> (*A History of Cadbury*)

Instead of working in fancy offices away from their workers, Richard and his brother worked in tiny cramped spaces and were constantly among their employees, working side-by-side. They would often take their breakfast in the factory as well, especially in the early days, and they started what was to become daily prayers. At first this was a reading from a suitable book followed by a few minutes of silent prayer and it grew into the daily morning prayers that continued for a long time at the factory, from Bridge Street to Bournville. These morning meetings remained in the memory of the workers for a long time to come. They were held in the girls' dining room and either Richard or George would lead a short service. They evolved to include a hymn at the start of every meeting, which was unusual in the Quaker faith, followed by a short reading from the Bible and summed up with a few words or a prayer.

Barrow remembered:

> *His faith was of the simplest, and by its simplicity he was the means of helping very many. He did not take great vocal part in our Friends' Meetings, but whenever he did speak it was with great concern and the message was one which he had much upon his mind. With Uncle George he shared the duties of reading at our morning meeting at the Works. The whole service, the hymn, the reading, the message and the prayer, took from seven to ten minutes. His remarks were often very helpful, and by their brevity were perhaps the more pointed.*
>
> (*Barrow Cadbury*)

Not many of the workers seem to have objected to this. In fact, it seems the opposite was the case. Employee William Cooper wrote:

> *Richard and George Cadbury made no secret of their trust in God in business as in all else. They took the risks of their faith. The short religious service held each morning was greatly valued by the workpeople with few exceptions.*
>
> *Some of these workpeople before leaving Bridge Street formed themselves into a committee with the purpose to take up social and religious work within the district surrounding Bournville.*
>
> *(Cadbury's Angels)*

It is not normal for Quakers to sing hymns at meetings, but both Richard and his brother encouraged this anyway. Vincent Grimnett was one worker who enjoyed this aspect. He remembered: *We became acquainted with some of the favourite hymns of Mr Richard and Mr George, 'Oh those clanging bells of time' was one of Mr George's. 'Go bury thy sorry', Mr Richard's. (Cadbury's Angels)*

On 17 May 1882, an article appeared in the *Gospel Temperance Herald*, referring to the brothers as 'Christian merchants of Birmingham', so well-known was their faith, and 'manufacturing princes', so well-known were their good hearts. The article is pasted into the family book with the date and the abbreviated journal title ('Gosp. Temp. Herald') written in Richard's hand, and it follows below:

> *MESSRS CADBURY BROTHERS, CHRISTIAN MERCHANTS OF BIRMINGHAM*
> *"The good alone have joy sincere,*
> *The good alone are great."*
> *AMONG the long list of Christian merchants and manufacturing princes of England, none are more widely known and respected than Messrs. Richard and George Cadbury of Birmingham. They have inherited very fine qualities from their honoured and revered father, who is still alive and in his 81st year, and who for more than half a century has taken an earnest interest in the welfare of the people. His two sons, of whom we now write, are walking*

in their father's footsteps, and are of one heart and one mind in all good religious and Temperance work. They are both in the prime of life, Richard, the eldest, being 46, and George 43.

Their early life and training were such as usually fall to the lot of the sons of the English middle classes. But we must not omit to notice that their father is a member of the Society of Friends, and both his sons hold the faith and practice of that honoured and revered society. Early in life they took to their father's business, which was then a small concern, employing about 30 work-people. Under their direction and control it has expanded and grown until now about 400 people are employed by them in the manufacture of high-class chocolate and cocoa essence.

Their new works at Bournville are a credit alike to their heads and hearts. Everything has been done that can be to add to the comfort, health and happiness of those employed in these factories. Exercise grounds are provided both for men and women, cooking arrangements for preparing the food of the employés, and a liberal supply of other conveniences can be found there. Every morning there is a short religious service held in a light airy room after breakfast. This service is usually conducted by one of the masters, and consists of singing, reading the Scriptures, and an address. It is held in the master's time, lasts about twenty minutes, and is much enjoyed by all who take part in it. Both Richard and George are connected with the Severn Street early Sunday morning school for men. Each one conducts a class in Board schools, and each brother has about 400 men in his division. The interest these two brothers take in this work can never be told. In all sorts of weather they can be seen walking to their school work at about seven o'clock on Sunday morning, an hour when many other business men are quietly resting in bed. They are always ready to help in the cause of Temperance, and liberally support it. They were the first to move in securing the services of Mr. R.T. Booth to carry on a Gospel Temperance Mission in Birmingham. The other day we paid a visit to their works, and saw a number of beautiful houses which they have erected for their work-people. These dwellings are models of neatness and quiet beauty. Each house is nestled in the midst of its own garden, and looks like a little paradise of comfort. Time and space would fail to tell of the many useful works to which they give their sympathy and practical help. George is a member of the Birmingham town council, and has the respect and love of his colleagues. But the Cadbury Brothers seek not for honour and glory in the arena of political strife and clamour. Their desire is to combat ignorance, to drive out darkness, to remove disorder, to destroy immorality, and usher in a better era of peace, sobriety, and righteousness. They find their happiness in making other people happy, their joy in helping others to be joyous, and their peace in living and teaching the principles of the Prince of Peace.

Both men would visit the work rooms often. Apparently, the cocoa moth was a bit of a nuisance, and if Richard knew there was one in the factory, he would not rest until it was gone, very often destroying the pest himself. Richard was known for his temper, which he could lose quite quickly, but should he ever find he was mistaken, he was equally as quick to go back and apologise to any injured party.

The brothers were both keen sportsmen and this carried over into the business. They were active members of the cricket team they formed at the works, and Richard was captain of both the football and hockey teams that played in Edgbaston during the 1850s. When it was possible, Richard and George and about twenty young men from the works would nip out to the fields and have a quick game of football or cricket. 'Country excursions were sometimes planned,' recounted Helen, 'and the firm was the first to introduce the Saturday half-holiday in Birmingham.'

Early in 1892, Richard Cadbury published a book entitled *Cocoa – all about it*, by "Historicus".

This was the first complete and comprehensive work ever published on the subject. The history and cultivation of the plant itself is first [explained]; then follows the history of its use as a food, with subsequent chapters on its analysis, manufacture, its value as an article of diet, and its adulterations.

[...] Its publication aroused a great deal of interest, and Richard Cadbury had taken infinite pains that it should be as attractively presented to the public as possible, not merely a learned dissertation on a food product and its manufacture. Almost every page is illustrated with coloured pictures, photographs, and engravings. Those which were most admired were the reproductions from quaint drawings in a rare work by Philippe Sylvestre Dufour, and one from an old Latin book on chocolate, allegorically representing a casket of chocolate being handed to Neptune to make known to the countries of the world. About three years later it became necessary to issue a new edition, which contained additional matter and new points of interest.

(Richard Cadbury of Birmingham)

A short introduction to the new edition follows:

Three years ago the writer ventured to place before the public some details respecting the cultivation and use of cocoa, and he has since been enabled to collect much new, and as he believes valuable, information. Few early books treat accurately or exhaustively of the subject, but nearly all the earlier travellers and settlers refer to cocoa as an important article of consumption in South America and Mexico, long before it was known in Europe. We owe much to adventurous navigators and explorers for luxuries that have now become a necessity of civilisation. Waste tracts of rich alluvial soil still remain uncultivated, and are likely, if properly utilised by generations to come, to be at once means of employment and sources of supply; it is generally admitted that cocoa claims probably more attention than any other food product throughout the tropical zone in which it flourishes.

(Cocoa – all about it, 2nd edition, 1896)

In this version of the book, Richard turned the story into a romantic adventure with Montezuma as the main hero.

It was 1879 when Richard's eldest son Barrow first came to the firm of Cadbury. During his holidays from college in Manchester, he assisted George H. Gadd, the architect who drew up the plans for the new factory at Bournville. He came to the firm on a permanent basis in 1882 and travelled to the United States and Canada on company business with William Tallis that same year. He was followed in 1887 by his younger brother William, once William had completed his apprenticeship with the German chocolate manufacturer Stollwerck in Cologne. And they were joined by their cousin, George Cadbury's son, George Jr, in 1897.

In January 1899, Richard and George drew up a new agreement. This agreement included converting the business to a private limited company should one of them die. Richard died only two months later and, on 13 June 1899, the company became known as Cadbury Brothers Ltd, with two of Richard's sons included in the board of directors. The firm had been a private venture for sixty-eight years.

Chapter 5

Family man

The loss of his mother in 1855 was a great blow to the young Richard Cadbury, but there was still much more sadness and grief to come. His older brother John had also recently been sent away for his health and was living in Herefordshire, learning farming. Their grandfather, Richard Tapper Cadbury, died in March 1860. In 1863, John left his farm and moved to the other side of the world with the intention of farming in Australia. In January 1866, younger brother Edward succumbed to a short illness. He was only 22 when he died. Then in May, John died of typhus in Brisbane. But this was not yet all, for in 1875, the youngest brother Henry died of typhoid fever, leaving a widow and a 3-month-old daughter. However, there was joy as well, for Richard Cadbury married his first wife, Elizabeth Adlington, on 24 July 1861.

Elizabeth was the daughter of William Adlington, a very well-known and much respected Quaker, and his wife Dorothy. She was born in Mansfield in 1838, the town in which they were married. She had received a good education and was very intelligent, as well as a skilled and accomplished seamstress. Elizabeth went to school with Richard's sister Maria in Lewes in Sussex. This school was owned by the three Dymond ladies, who were also Friends. She was the sister of a friend of Richard's too, from his days at Benjamin Abbot's Quaker school in Hitchin. They were married at a Friends' meeting in Mansfield.

'Elizabeth was a bright, vivacious girl, slim and graceful in figure, and with a sweet, intelligent face,' wrote Helen Cadbury Alexander in her biography of her father. 'She was accomplished and well informed, a good conversationalist, and had attractive manners.' She was also a member of the Society of Friends.

Wheeley's Road

Richard moved his new bride into 17 Wheeley's Road, Edgbaston, where he laid out a beautiful garden with a rockery for the various specimens that had thus far resided next to the pond in his father's garden in Calthorpe Road. On 8 April 1861, Richard wrote a letter to his younger brother Henry, who was away at school in Kendal at the time: *My little house is beginning to look charming now it is nearly completed; it will, however, find me plenty to do to buy furniture for it. I have had a boat-load of rockery put on to the bank by the canal, so that I hope to make that respectable before I have done.*

Later that same month, Richard and his brother George took over at the family works in Bridge Street. The shop John Cadbury had opened in Bull Street thirty years earlier was now in the hands of his nephew, the boys' cousin, Richard Cadbury Barrow.

Named for his grandmother's family, Richard's first son Barrow Cadbury was born on 27 September 1862 at Wheeley's Road. He remembered:

> *My earliest picture is of the little Quaker home into which I was born. I can recollect that as a little boy, my coat had only one button at the neck. I must have looked rather like the pictures of a charity boy!*
>
> (*Barrow Cadbury*)

He would also remember this house with the garden that went all the way down to the canal. The eldest Cadbury child would play on the banks of the canal and he believed that this was where his father hid his money. A sister, Alice, was born in 1864, but she died seven months later. She was buried in the burial ground of the Friends' Meeting House in Leominster, as the family were visiting relations at the time that she died. Another sister, Jessie, was born in 1865, and she survived. William came along in 1867, to be followed by Richard Junior in 1868.

Like her husband, Elizabeth Adlington Cadbury was interested in the welfare of the people who worked at the firm, in her case the girls, and she would often visit any who fell ill. However, in December 1868, on New Year's Eve and only ten days after the birth of their youngest child, Elizabeth died. Richard was left with these four small children.

Richard was to write of his wife: *Her life was one that left an example to her children and others of modesty, purity, and truthfulness; with but little outward show, she was a humble-minded Christian, acknowledging Christ as her all-sufficient Saviour, in whom we believe she has now found perfect rest. (Richard Cadbury of Birmingham)*

And Jessie wrote of her father at this time:

His tender love for his children has been ever the same. He was everything to our baby lives. I can well remember riding on his shoulder, and going to him with our troubles; he was so much to us always. We loved the tales which he told to all his children in turn. If only they had been written down they would charm many a child, so simple, sweet, and full of mischief and fun. It is wonderful when one recalls the sorrow he went through, and how he was pressed with business and philanthropic work, how he always found time for his children. Even on Sunday, though very busy with mission work, he never missed giving us those never-to-be-forgotten Bible lessons and talks. He often broke down in his tender longing that his children should be followers of God. I remember now the drawings he made with pencil to illustrate a point when he thought it would help us more clearly to understand. His tenderness in reproving us when we were older, and the remembrance of his gentle sadness when we had done wrong, brings tears to one's eyes even now. Perhaps the knowledge of his justice, as well as his love for us, was one great fact that made him such a real friend to his children. Amongst so many of us there were, of course, different dispositions, as well as a great variety of ability; yet he never showed partiality, and we felt that the same real love existed for each. To be enwrapped in our father's tender embrace made one feel it was worth while braving anything.

(Richard Cadbury of Birmingham)

William Cadbury was not even 2 years old when his mother died, but he did remember being lifted up in her arms so that he could see a candlestick on the mantelpiece. He also remembered being told that if he planted a penny in the garden, a rose tree would grow. Being a lover of red roses, he did indeed plant a penny and a red rose tree did grow ... but he also spotted a neighbour brandishing a trowel. This fairytale was probably told to William by his grandfather, as he was sent to live with John Cadbury, and his aunt Maria, when his mother died.

In remembering his mother, Barrow wrote:

> *I have somewhere a statement of Father's income during the early years of their struggle soon after I was born. I well remember Father saying how when my mother was far from well he took her to Pebble Mill where there was a pretty stream, and how they had to tramp all the way back again, when he would have given so much, had he possessed it, to take her home in a cab.*
>
> *(Barrow Cadbury)*

Richard met Emma Jane Wilson in 1870 and it has been suggested that it was love at first sight.

Emma Jane was born in Greet in Birmingham on Christmas Day in 1846. She was one of seven children and was only 15 when her father died. Before his death her father had invested heavily in the railways and had lost a great deal of his money. His wife, and later widow, was forced to find alternative means with which to keep their family, so she turned to tutoring. In fact, she taught all of her own children herself. Shortly after her husband's death, in 1869, Emma Wilson Senior met Richard Cadbury. A kind-hearted yet practical woman, she needed a way to support herself and her seven children and Richard had recently opened a day nursery for the children of working women. Richard was also still grieving for the wife who had died in 1869, leaving him with four children of his own. The two had much in common and soon Emma Sr was working with him, both at the crèche, or children's day centre, and in his home looking after his children. In fact, he asked her to run the crèche in Bishopsgate Street. It was to be the first of its kind in England. (See Chapter 8.)

The day nursery really was something quite new. In October 1870, Richard wrote in a letter to Emma Jane:

I called at the children's Day Nursery this evening and saw the mothers coming for their children. It really did me good to see how pleased they seemed at finding them so happy, and with clean faces too, which is a blessing many of them were total strangers to before.

Then in February 1871, a reporter from one of the newspapers in Birmingham dropped in on Richard Cadbury to talk about the crèche. His editor was keen to include an article about the day nursery as he thought it would be a good idea to open more of the nurseries in other parts of Birmingham.

In the holidays, two of Emma's children would often come to the house to stay with their mother, and in 1870, Emma Jane arrived home from Switzerland. Emma Jane was away at school in Switzerland when her mother started to work with Richard Cadbury, and when she was due to return home, Mrs Wilson asked Richard if her daughter might move in with them for the time being while she looked for alternative accommodation. Richard agreed, and Emma arrived at Wheeley's Road in the autumn. When she rang the doorbell, it was Richard who opened the door. Within a month, they were engaged to be married.

Although they were both of different religions, and despite the age gap (he was 35 and she was 23 when they were married), the couple had a lot in common. They both enjoyed travel, they both loved Switzerland equally, and Emma was also very fond of children. They announced their engagement in the October, and Richard wrote to Emma: *I have told my brothers and sister today, and they are perfectly satisfied with the step I have taken.*

For the sake of propriety, Richard moved out of the house in Wheeley's Road because Emma was still living there with her mother. During this separation and their temporarily secret engagement, Richard and Emma corresponded prolifically. While many letters were exchanged between the pair, Emma's are apparently lost, but Richard's give some insight into what life was like for the family in those days. In 1906, Helen Alexander, Richard's daughter, wrote a biography of her father, and she included some of these letters. A lot of what was

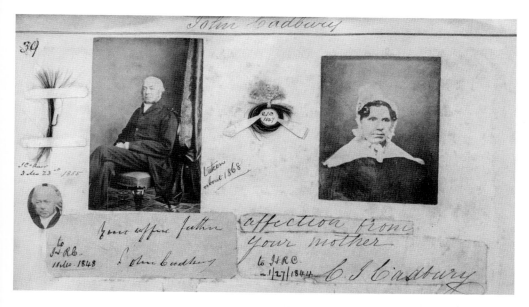

Above: A page from the family book. The title at the top of the page, John Cadbury, is in Richard's writing. The writing on the left is John Cadbury's, "to J & RC" (to John and Richard Cadbury), and was written in 1848. The writing on the right is their mother's, dated 1844. There is a lock of John Cadbury's hair, taken in 1855 and tied with a piece of string, and a lock of Candia's hair, taken in 1847 and tied with ribbon. (*From the collection of the Library of the Society of Friends (Quakers) in Britain*)

Right: John Cadbury with his daughter, Richard's sister, Maria, in 1879. (*From the collection of the Library of the Society of Friends (Quakers) in Britain*)

Richard with his sister Maria and his brother George. George is still wearing a dress, as was the norm in those days until the child was "dry". (*Taken from* Richard Cadbury of Birmingham, *with kind permission from the family*)

(Left to right) Richard Cadbury, aged 17, John Cadbury Jr, aged 18½, and Maria Cadbury, aged 14, taken in the autumn of 1852. (*From the collection of the Library of the Society of Friends (Quakers) in Britain*)

Above and below: The family book, known as *The Cadbury Pedigree*, is being cared for at Friends House, Euston, London. (© *Ian Wordsworth. With permission from the Library of the Society of Friends (Quakers) in Britain*)

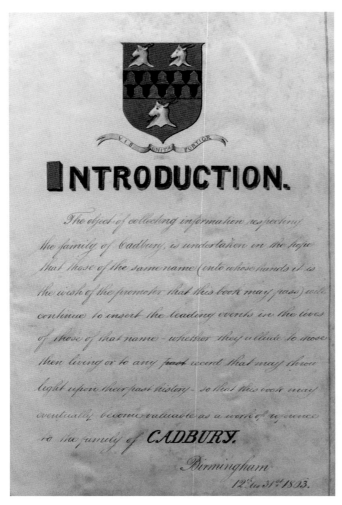

INTRODUCTION.

The object of collecting information respecting the family of Cadbury, is undertaken in the hope that those of the same name (into whose hands it is the wish of the promoter that this book may pass) will continue to insert the leading events in the lives of those of that name – whether they allude to those then living or to any past event that may throw light upon their past history – so that this book may eventually become valuable as a work of reference to the family of **CADBURY.**

Birmingham
12th to 31st 1803.

Left: The title page from the family book. (*From the collection of the Library of the Society of Friends (Quakers) in Britain*)

Below: Richard Cadbury spent many holidays learning about his ancestors, who were tenant farmers in Devon. He often sketched and painted pictures of the houses the families were thrown out of. (*From the collection of the Library of the Society of Friends (Quakers) in Britain*)

A page in the family book showing the Crooked Lane property after it had been rebuilt in 1858, and the old chocolate manufactory that was pulled down in 1847, the latter sketched from memory by Richard Cadbury, and of the shop in Bull Street in 1856. There is also a flyer dated 1845. (*From the collection of the Library of the Society of Friends (Quakers) in Britain*)

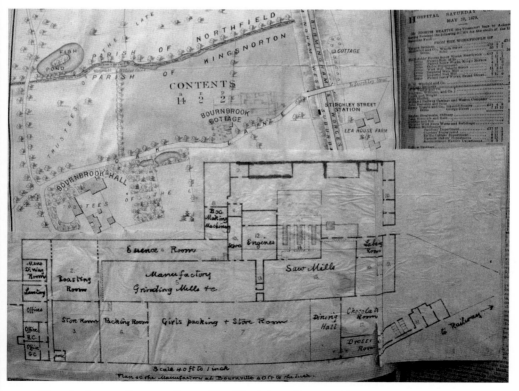

Plans for the new factory at Bournville. (*From the collection of the Library of the Society of Friends (Quakers) in Britain*)

Above left: The first ever chocolate box illustration was based on this painting by Richard Cadbury. Richard has written on this: "The original was painted in the spring of 1868." (*From the collection of the Library of the Society of Friends (Quakers) in Britain*)

Above right: Another chocolate box illustration was based on this painting by Richard Cadbury. Richard has written on this one: "The originals of Nos. 1, 2, & 3 were painted in the autumn of 1868. R.C." This one was no 1. (*From the collection of the Library of the Society of Friends (Quakers) in Britain*)

This was another chocolate box design originally painted by Richard Cadbury that also featured on the cover of *Cadbury's Angels* by Iris Carrington. (*Reproduced with kind permission from the family*)

Above: A page from the family book. The photographs are of Richard Cadbury and his first wife, Elizabeth, both taken in 1861. The writing on the left is Richard's, while the writing on the right is Elizabeth's, both dated 1864. There is a lock of Richard Cadbury's hair, and a lock of Elizabeth's hair, both taken in 1866 and tied with what looks like green wool. (*From the collection of the Library of the Society of Friends (Quakers) in Britain*)

Right: Richard Cadbury's sons: (top, left to right) Barrow, 1882; William, 1880. (bottom) Richard, 1876. (*Taken from* Richard Cadbury of Birmingham, *with kind permission from the family*)

Richard Cadbury and Emma Wilson, taken at about the time of their marriage in 1871. (*Taken from* Richard Cadbury of Birmingham, *with kind permission from the family*)

Richard's daughters: (left to right) Helen, Jessie, Edith, Margaret. (front) Beatrice. Picture taken 1888. (*From the collection of the Library of the Society of Friends (Quakers) in Britain*)

Blue plaque on the side of Richard Cadbury's house in Wheeley's Road, Edgbaston. (© *Ian Wordsworth. With permission from the current occupiers*)

The works at Bournville today. (© *Ian Wordsworth*)

Moseley Hall as it looks today. It is currently a hospital. (© Ian Wordsworth)

Richard and Emma Cadbury surrounded by all of Richard's children. (back) Barrow, Richard Jr, Edith, William, Margaret, Richard. (front) Helen, Jessie, Beatrice, Emma. (*With kind permission from the family*)

Above left: George and Richard Cadbury, 1896. (*Taken from* Richard Cadbury of Birmingham, *with kind permission from the family*)

Above right: Richard with his youngest daughter, Beatrice, 1890. (*Reproduced with kind permission from the family*)

Uffculme today. (© *Ian Wordsworth*)

Beatrice and her cousin Alec. (*Taken from* Richard Cadbury of Birmingham, *with kind permission from the family*)

Emma and Richard on the occasion of their silver wedding anniversary. (*Taken from* Richard Cadbury of Birmingham, *with kind permission from the family*)

Above: The almshouses
in Bournville today.
(© *Ian Wordsworth*)

Right: Richard Cadbury.
(*Reproduced with kind permission
from the family*)

Rowing on the River Jordan, probably 1897. (*Taken from* Richard Cadbury of Birmingham, *with kind permission from the family*)

Next to the Dead Sea. The gentleman in the middle with the snowy beard would be Richard Cadbury. Probably 1897. (*Taken from* Richard Cadbury of Birmingham, *with kind permission from the family*)

A bedroom tent in Palestine, 1897. (*Taken from* Richard Cadbury of Birmingham, *with kind permission from the family*)

Richard and Emma Cadbury strolling hand-in-hand on the sand at Port Said, 1897. (*Taken from* Richard Cadbury of Birmingham, *with kind permission from the family*)

The grave of Richard and Emma Cadbury in Lodge Hill Cemetery today, who died in 1899 and 1907 respectively. (© *Ian Wordsworth*)

Richard Cadbury
1835 – 1899, from a painting by Percy Bigland, June 1925. No copyright restrictions known.
(*Used with permission from Richard Cadbury's great-granddaughter Mary Penny*)

contained in the correspondence was personal and intimate in nature, but below are some less personal extracts from those letters, arranged by topic rather than in chronological order:

Extracts from letters from Richard Cadbury to Emma Jane Wilson:
[Of their engagement ...]

22 October 1870

I have felt happier to-day than for a long time. Your dear mother seemed not only satisfied but really happy, in the thought that we love each other as we do. I have told my father and brothers and sister to-day, and they are perfectly satisfied with the step I have taken. I can assure you of a very warm welcome from them all.

10 November 1870

I feel how heartily you have entered into the thought of fulfilling the duties of a wife, and I may also say of a mother of the little motherless ones, and feel assured that God will help you to fulfil your trust. I am so glad of your letters, which breathe so much love to me. They are like so many stepping stones across a broad river, until I meet you once again in that land of bright and happy days.

18 April 1871

My sister is looking forward with great pleasure to being one of your bridesmaids. The children will be near home while we are away, perhaps at Castle Bromwich.

13 July 1871

Last Sunday was almost, if not quite, the very happiest day in my life, and particularly as we sat together in church, and sang those beautiful hymns; shall we not often have as happy a time together? For the whole soul and heart seems to join together in one aspiration of praise. When we are together, dearest, on the ocean of life, there will be many rough waves to cross, many stiff gales to encounter; but if we place our trust in the Heavenly Pilot, He will lead us safely into the haven of rest and peace.

[Of family life ...]

28 October 1870

The children were all in the nursery together, Barrow doing his best to dress Willie, and Bonny [Richard Jr] *reaching out for a frock which he would insist on as being necessary to complete his toilet, although quite dressed. Jessie, who was glad to receive the last 'touches up', was enjoying a warm fire, and wanted to know all about the morning's bustle. Barrow and Jessie went with me to Calthorpe Street* [John Cadbury's home] *to dine, and were very happy with some new toys their auntie* [Maria] *had been buying for them.*

2 November 1870

Barrow and Jessie came downstairs this morning quite full of pleasure, to tell me about the two little French Dolls, Eugène and Marguerite, which you so kindly dressed for them, and which are pretty indeed.

26 November 1870

The children are very well. Barrow is getting on nicely with his lessons; Jessie is lively and affectionate; Willie, "the little brother," is beginning to show real progress with his reading; and Bonny is as sweet as ever.

29 December 1870

The canal is frozen quite hard. It was a great delight to Barrow and Jessie to have a run and slide with me as far as the tunnel.

25 January 1871

I have never told you how much I admire the scrap-book you have made for the children, and which has given them a great deal of pleasure already. Some day I shall have them round me and tell them some tales out of it. The first picture reminds me very much of you; I do not mean in likeness, but in mind, for you would be such a loving nurse. [It was a picture of a nurse.]

14 February 1871
Dear little Barrow went off to school yesterday; his lips quivered a little as he said good-bye, but he bore up bravely, and in the evening, when nurse took some clothes, etc., he wrote me a little note to say that he was very happy. There were a lot of Valentines for the children this morning, and they were much delighted.

21 February 1871
Dear little Barrow has been very happy at school. He was very much pleased to go with me to his Bible class on Sunday morning. I am so glad he takes an interest in these things. Yesterday I attended the meeting of the Men's class I sometimes teach on Sunday [this is the adult school in Severn Street]. *There were about seventy or eighty there, and when I was comfortably seated to enjoy hearing others talk, I was called upon the first to make a speech. I was not prepared, but I said a few words, commending their report, and then we had some capital addresses from other gentlemen, and many of the scholars themselves. To-day another class, numbering probably four hundred, will meet in the same room at Severn Street.*

28 February 1871
Jessie was admiring some of her curls this morning, and remarked that they would soon look like yours, so you see you have another admirer among us. She is such a merry little thing.

18 April 1871
Barrow has had ten days' holiday which he has much enjoyed, and returned to school yesterday.

[Of the war in France ...]
2 November 1870
Is it not sad to be expecting to hear of the general bombardment of Paris by any telegram?

25 January 1871
Poor France – her troubles do not seem at an end at present.

28 February 1871
I am sending you a paper giving an account of the Continent. It is a good thing that this fearful war is over for the present, but what wretchedness and misery will be left behind after the troops are cleared away. No earthly blessing can replace the loss of fathers slain on the battlefield to their poor widows left with their little ones, in many cases turned out from their homes, and all they had in this world taken away and destroyed. I will try and send you L'International, *as it gives French ideas on the subject.*

21 March 1871
I have sent you to-day's paper, because it contains so much of interest, including Napoleon's arrival in England and the fearful rioting in Paris.

23 March 1871
The news from Paris this evening is fearful; the nation seems to have gone wild.

4 April 1871
William Sturge has gone to Nantes, and then on to the valley of the Loire, where Friends are distributing a large quantity of seed to the farmers, who have none to sow their land with; and it is believed that this is the best means of helping them to help themselves in the fearful condition they were left in by the war. What fearful accounts there are from Paris. I hope you will like the French papers I send you; some of the accounts are most graphic.

[Of religion ...]
6 November 1870
I have begun to read the Church Services, and will tell you more when we meet. It is such a comfort to me to have the

prospect of joining you in worship next Sunday. It seems such a bond of union for the soul, to worship together the one great Father of all; and although I cannot understand the efficacy of priestly ordinations, yet it makes me very happy to think that we can both own the one great Sacrifice for sin, through whom alone *we can find atonement and by whom* alone *we can approach God's mercy seat (Heb. vii. 26-28).*

I went to our first Essay Meeting on Friday. There were some capital essays – one on "Fashionable Quakers" was most spirited. About forty-eight were present, and nine essays were read. I shall feel proud to take you some of these days, and introduce you in the social gatherings to some whom I think you will like.

15 November 1870

In our conversation together you asked me respecting our disuse of ritual service in the Society of Friends, and I told you that I thought it might be better not to trouble you about such things at present; but I have since thought that perhaps you would be puzzling yourself over it, and wondering how as a Christian, professing my entire belief in the Scriptures as the Word of God, I could omit them. If it would be any comfort to you, I will gladly write them down for you in a simple way. Religion seems to me such a work of God's Holy Spirit in the heart, that although we may reverently thank Him for many ways in which Christ has been revealed to us as the only means by which our guilt can be washed away, yet these can be of no avail unless blessed by the great Giver, and unless we open the door of our hearts to receive Him, who has been knocking there until "His head is filled with dew and His locks with the drops of the night." This is the glorious promise: "If any man hear My voice and open the door, I will come in to him and sup with him and he with Me." With what joy, then, shall we open the gates for the Lord of Glory to enter in. I shall always think of this when I read the beautiful piece we sang together, "Abide with me".

31 January 1871

I read the collect [in the Book of Common Prayer] *you spoke of in your letter and thought it a very beautiful one. How often we need to be reminded that this is not our rest, and that while we are here temptations and trials will be our lot [...] Your love and your religious faith have drawn me very near to you, and if it be still God's will that different paths are chosen for us to the one source of everlasting joy, we shall be sure to meet there, and perhaps in God's love and mercy He may still see fit to join us in the same path, for some steps of our earthly pilgrimage, before we meet on that heavenly shore.*

7 February 1871

I have been reading the Twenty-seventh Psalm this evening; it is a beautiful one. What a never-failing source of joy for the Christian to know that, whatever may befall him on this earth, he can trust in One who is able to deliver to the uttermost.

14 February 1871

I have just returned from our first temperance meeting, and am now sitting down for a quiet hour with you. We had both rooms crowded, and some first-rate speeches made by working men, interspersed by recitations and songs. There were several of the very worst class there and I believe that even thinking of you often strengthens me in desiring to do my best. I expect they will want me to take the chair again.

21 February 1871

Thank you for the little book; it is very nice to read anything of the kind, where the spirit is dictated by a Christian, who would win souls for Christ. I wish that all Christians could see alike as to the way to worship their Creator; it does seem strange, but if it be God's ordering for some good purpose we cannot now see, we must be content. We now only look through a glass darkly, but then face to face. It is a certain bond for the Christian to know that at the best *our worship is imperfect, because God's presence is not fully revealed. It is a bond because it links every true Christian in the chain of sympathy and love.*

21 March 1871
We do not have any Meeting on Good Friday, because I believe Friends generally think that all days are alike holy, except those especially appointed in the Bible, as the Sabbath, which is to be entirely dedicated to the Lord. I do not think we can devote too much time or too many days to good works and thoughts, when we consider how short a time our life is here, to prepare for an eternal life above; but there is, I think, very likely a danger in man *appointing any day for* others *as holier than the rest.*

31 March 1871
I like a great deal in the little book you so kindly sent me, and which I have read through carefully. I have made one or two notes explaining what points I cannot see with the author; not that I say I am right and he is wrong. There is only one part that I do grieve over, and that is where the bread and wine *are treated as "holy mysteries," as being "the means" by which God's grace is* "conveyed" *or* communicated, *instead of being taken as a* reminder *according to the generally accepted meaning of the words, "Do this in remembrance of me."*

4 April 1871
I have just returned from a Temperance meeting at the Town Hall, and heard some most telling speeches from good and earnest men – two Baptist ministers, a Roman Catholic clergyman, and an Archdeacon from the Established Church were among the speakers.

9 May 1871
There are a great many children in the day nursery; one day last week they had thirty-eight, and could have had four more. Poor little Esther Dyson is still living,

and the doctors think she may partially recover. It is so delightful to sit by her as she lies in bed, and to hear her speak of peace and rest in Jesus. I have often thought how comforting it would be if one of my own dear little ones was dying, if they could look forward with such joy to the blessed change.

16 May 1871
I had a very nice little meeting last Sunday at the day nursery. Five or six earnest men joined us from another place of worship, and three appeared in supplication, praying most earnestly for the poor widows, that they might have consolation, and for the drunkards, that they might see the error of their ways. My reading was the first part of the eighteenth chapter of Matthew, where Christ shows His disciples that they must be as humble and as pure in spirit as a little child.

23 May 1871
I do so like your way of speaking on the points of doctrine on which we may differ. Do excuse me, dearest, if I have written too positively on any points, for I would be as Paul admonishes Timothy to be – "the servant of the Lord must not strive, but be gentle unto all men, apt to teach, patient."

16 June 1871
In prayer we may rest on the care of One who is mighty to save, so that when thoughts trouble us, or when even mingled feelings oppress us, it is a great comfort to have full trust in the assurance that He will do all things well.

[Of the new house on Wheeley's Hill ...]
23 November 1870
I have just been with my father to look over one of the new houses that are nearly finished on the right-hand side of Wheeley's Hill. Everything seems complete and beautifully arranged. Father is anxious that I should secure it. Do you think you would like the situation?

FAMILY MAN

26 November 1870
I have again been over the house in Wheeley's Road, with your
dear mother, who likes it very much, and thinks you would too.
How happy it makes me to think of everything nice for you.

7 February 1871
It is difficult to say when we shall move into the new house,
for so much has to be done, and the weather has been so cold
that the men have not done the work they would have. [...]
The woods will soon begin to look lovely. There is always
such a joyous feeling in springtime. The birds wake up to a
new life, and all is new again.

21 March 1871
We are in a glorious state of muddle this evening, in
preparation for a grand move to-morrow. My greatest
pleasure now is to do what I know you will like me to do. Do
you not sometimes yourself feel a secret pleasure in giving
up some little enjoyment to please those you love? I know
that we both do, so you need never be afraid of telling me
all you think.

It makes things feel more like a reality now that we are
really moving, and I try to fancy you as mistress of our little
domain.

9 May 1871
We so much enjoy the delicious green of the young leaves
and grass. It is such a pretty view along the canal, with the
peep through the tunnel. The may is just beginning to show
itself among the bushes on the banks.

[Of life at work ...]
25 January 1871
We have been having a good deal of the cocoa that was
shipped from Le Havre to Liverpool.

31 January 1871
My brother George was in Liverpool yesterday and bought
a large quantity of cocoa that usually goes to France.

Henry is in the Isle of Wight, so I have it to myself, and as we are very busy it keeps me close at work.

14 February 1871
We had about thirty-five [valentines] *among our letters to-day for the girls at the warehouse; some were quite large packages, but we kept them all till just before they went, or there would have been a great deal of time wasted. As it was there was such a rush for them, and excitement, that it was not easy for the forewoman to distribute them to the rightful owners.*

4 April 1871
Father has invited me to breakfast with Archdeacon Sandford, who is staying at Calthorpe Street. He is such an interesting old man, with a long, silvery beard. I do not think I shall be able to go, because I take the reading in the mornings for the people at the warehouse; and as they gather over two hundred sometimes, I cannot leave it to any one.

25 April 1871
I have just finished two more little paintings for the oval chocolate boxes, and intend to do one more. Would you like to see them before I send them to be engraved from?

16 June 1871
I was so exulting in the prospect of coming over on Tuesday to see you, when I remembered that it was impossible. Both my brothers, George and Henry, will be away on important and necessary business, and I am left alone in charge. I fear "patience" is hardly a virtue with me now, excepting so far as it is a necessity.

[Of life in general ...]
14 February 1871
A gentleman from one of the Birmingham papers called on me to-day to say that the editor was anxious to write an

*article upon my day nursery, as it was almost unknown, and he thought it would be very useful to establish several of the same kind in other parts of the town. The piece of fern you sent me made quite a lovely little valentine, with the snowdrops on it. The snowdrop is the emblem of consolation. The fern is the "Prickly fern" (*Polipodium aculeatum*), and is one of our prettiest species. It is almost an evergreen, too, which makes it charming to have through the winter; but to look as bright as the specimen you sent, it requires to be in a shady place and a fine loamy soil.*

2 May 1871
I have taken Mr. Laundy's Bible class at the Friends' Mission Rooms this evening. I do so enjoy having a class of men; they are so intelligent, and enter into the interest of the thing so.

23 May 1871
Barrow is very happy at school. It is such a pleasure to have him at home on Saturday and Sunday, and is also a great treat to the others, who cling to him, and think much of their "big brother at school."

13 June 1871
I was so glad to have your letter on Sunday morning, although I did not get it until after Meeting, for I took a class at our school in Severn Street, and then Barrow and Jessie met me, and we walked down to Meeting together. Can you do without me until Monday, do you think? For though I am impatient to see you again, I should be able to have my little meeting on Sunday at the day nursery. We had such a nice gathering yesterday, that with the prospect of being away three or four Sundays, I do not like to leave them.

1 July 1871
I am so glad that you have spent such a pleasant evening at Mr. Fry's. I saw the two elder boys at Calthorpe Street

when they were there. Barrow and the eldest boy had a game together, and I thought how curious it would be if they were to become rivals in the same trade. I fear sometimes I appear to you much better than I am, but you will find a great many faults, a great many "little foxes"; but I will strive to overcome them, dearest, and with your love I believe, I shall.

Less than a year after they first met, Richard and Emma were married on 25 July 1871, in the Anglican church in Bristol. Her sisters Hannah and Alice and Richard's sister Maria were bridesmaids. Richard's brothers George and Henry and Emma's mother Emma Sr were also present but unfortunately, Richard's father, John Cadbury, was unable to be there due to his poor health. However, on their way to their honeymoon in the Lake District, the newlyweds managed to meet him as they passed though the Birmingham station. John Cadbury had with him a basket of grapes for their journey and a purse of gold for his new daughter-in-law.

There are three railway stations in Birmingham, two of which were built at this time, and only one originally known as the Birmingham station. That was renamed Snow Hill Station in the late 1850s. The story of her parents' wedding was recollected by their daughter Helen in her book in 1906 and then later by their youngest daughter Beatrice after her sister's death in 1969, so probably in the 1970s. Snow Hill Station was closed in 1968 but reopened in 1987. Until its closure, it was still an important mainline station, as it had always been. Therefore, it can be assumed that it was Snow Hill Station where Richard and Emma met with John Cadbury on their honeymoon journey.

Emma's older brother Ashlin was a travelling man who went to Brazil. On one of his home visits he had brought with him a parrot called Polly, who very quickly became a favourite of Richard Cadbury's. She would screechingly greet him each morning until he took her out of her cage and petted her. Then he would give her a treat and put her back in her cage. Later, when the family was much bigger, Polly would perch on the youngest Cadbury's shoulder taking sweet treats from her hand.

Literally overnight, Emma became both wife to Richard and mother to his children – Barrow, William, Jessie and Richard Jr. Despite their different religious beliefs, for some time Emma would accompany her new husband to meetings on a Sunday morning, and he would go with her to a Church of England service of an evening. However, within two years of their wedding, and of her own volition, Emma joined the Society of Friends.

Wheeley's Hill (later also known as part of Wheeley's Road)

In around 1872, in what was once a field opposite the famous anti-slavery campaigner Joseph Sturge's house, a short distance from where Richard lived, were built some new houses. It had always been known as Sturge's Field, in which members of the public were permitted by the owner to enjoy some relaxation time. But now the field was being built upon and the houses had long gardens that ran down to the canal. This was before the railway came and the canal was as wide as a river.

Richard decided he would have one of these houses, and he wrote in a letter to Emma: *We have not quite decided about making a boathouse, for they say that the railway company, who have an Act for carrying a line along the canal on the other side, will make it only half the width, which would spoil it for rowing.*

About a year after they moved into the new house on Wheeley's Hill, baby Edith came along and joined her older half-siblings.

By now, Richard's eldest son Barrow was almost 11 years old, and his father wanted him to have as wide an education as possible, as he himself had done. He was particularly keen for Barrow to learn a foreign language and experience life in a foreign country. Richard and Emma were carrying out some family research in Devonshire when a German lady happened to be staying with John and Maria Cadbury. Emily Kölle had been a governess for many years and was now widowed with a little boy of her own. She didn't teach any children herself any longer, but she did allow a few English boys to stay at her home in Stuttgart while they attended a day school in the town. John wrote to his son and daughter-in-law on 9 August 1873:

> *MY DEAR SON AND DAUGHTER, – Emily Kölle and her son are pleasantly staying with us; we find them most cheerful company. I much want to lay before you the subject that has arisen during our intercourse with Emily Kölle. She has settled to take under her care the*

son of Edward Crossfield, the son of George Dymond, and also the son of Henry Ellis, – a first-rate opportunity for these youths to obtain a thorough knowledge of the German language, and to be under the judicious and motherly care of Emily Kölle. It make me long that dear Barrow should share in this high privilege. She considers he is exactly the right age, and would in a year or two obtain a thorough knowledge of German, and at the same time a sound education at one of the excellent schools at Stuttgart. Please do seriously think this matter over before you return.

Richard and Emma did indeed consider the matter before they returned home, and in due course, on his eleventh birthday, Barrow Cadbury sailed with Frau Kölle and her son to Germany. The following summer, Maria accompanied her brother and sister-in-law on a visit to Stuttgart, travelling on to Ragatz in Switzerland. It was here that Richard painted many of the pictures that would later adorn the Cadbury's chocolate boxes.

Not long after they returned from visiting Barrow in Germany, the family moved house again.

Harborne Road

John Cadbury lived in a large house on Calthorpe Road, which had been extended and added to over the years. But by now, with all of his sons married and moved out, the house was far too big for him and his daughter Maria. At the back of this house was a large field that looked onto Harborne Road. John had two houses built on this field, both with good-sized gardens, although John and Maria moved into the one that still held some of the fruit trees. The pool was still in this garden too, along with many of the ferns that Richard had brought home from his travels. Richard and his new wife moved into the other house and all of his children could play together in the gardens.

Parts of the old home lived on in these gardens: *The garden was still spacious, and contained memorials of the old home – a part of the orchard, and the pool with its rock island, where grew the ferns brought*

by the children in the old days from the farm at Scalemire and elsewhere.
(*Life of George Cadbury*)

It was while the family lived here that Richard's younger brother Henry, who had joined the firm in 1869, contracted typhoid fever. He died at the end of 1875, leaving a wife and child.

Richard built a Swiss chalet at the bottom of the garden in Harborne Road. The lower half of this chalet was more like a tool shed where the boys' bicycles and gardening implements were stored. Richard was a very keen gardener and could be found working there early in the mornings or in the evenings. The second storey had green-shuttered windows, and the family would often enjoy a picnic in this room.

Two more daughters were born while Richard and his family lived in Harborne Road. Helen was born on 10 January 1877 and Margaret (Daisy) was born on 19 November 1878. Richard's eldest daughter with Emma, Edith, was a little sickly, and the doctor suggested she should live close to the sea. In 1882, Edith was sent to school at Weston-super-Mare. Then Richard's youngest son with Elizabeth, who was 14 by now, was sent to live with Frau Kölle in Stuttgart, as Barrow had been. Barrow by now was back home in England but had gone to school in Manchester for a year.

The house on Harborne Road turned out to be a long way from the factory at Bournville and even further from the mission hall in Highgate.

Chapter 6

Moseley Hall, Uffculme, and the family book

Moseley Hall

Moseley in Birmingham isn't very far from the Edgbaston Cricket Ground where Warwickshire County Cricket Club have their home and Test Matches are also played. Dating back to the *Domesday Book*, Moseley was still a village in the mid-nineteenth century, surrounded by fields and trees.

The industrial centre of Birmingham was 3 miles to the north. Moseley Hall was rebuilt in around 1795, having been burned to the ground in 1791 during the Priestley Riots. The Priestley Riots were also known as the Birmingham Riots and they took place during July 1791. The rioters' targets were, funnily enough, religious dissenters who had split away from the Church of England and, in particular, the famous dissenter and separatist Joseph (J.B.) Priestley, who had lived at Moseley Hall. From about 1852, following the then owner's death, the hall was leased out.

Moseley was about equidistant from both the new works at Bournville and the mission in Highgate. In those days it was still considered the countryside and the children listened to their father's tales of the place with excitement.

Richard moved the family to Moseley Hall in 1883, buying it outright in 1889. Helen and Daisy were 7 and 6 years old when the family moved in. Helen Cadbury remembered the move very well, although she did so in the third person:

> [The children would] *never forget the happy day when all preparations were at last complete, and they drove away,*

leaving behind the pretty roads of Edgbaston, lined with houses and gardens. What seemed to their excited fancy an immensely long drive brought them at last by the country high-road to the village green of Moseley. Round the green were low houses and old-fashioned shops, with a blacksmith's at the corner, and up a street to the left could be seen the square tower of the village church. Close by the green, and sloping steeply from the road at right angles, was the entrance to Moseley Hall. Tall wooden gates, flanked by a little lodge on each side, were thrown open under the shade of spreading trees, and showed a vista of the long drive, winding between woods and fields, down-hill and up again, with glimpses of the pool in the bottom of the valley. The old house, with its portico of stone pillars, its spacious rooms, and long, stone-paved passages, was full of mystery and delight to the young folks. [...] The cellars, much older than the rest of the building, stretched under the whole length, and the fact that some of them were built for prisons and had been used for this purpose gave to explorations through them a weird and mysterious charm.

(Richard Cadbury of Birmingham)

Moseley has certainly changed a lot since then, and so has Moseley Hall. Now the house is part of a hospital, with extensions and extra buildings added all around it. The portico is still there, and so is the long winding drive. Most of the woods and lawns are now car parks, and you have to walk around what seems to be the back of the old building to see what is actually the front. There is a mark above the portico of pillars, across its whole length, that looks as though there was another structure protruding from beneath the upstairs windows, and this may have been the case long before Richard Cadbury moved there but photographs taken in the late 1800s show that there was nothing there by this time. The paths are still lined with bushes and trees, with some shielding the house from the main road – and it is a very busy main road – and at least one of the car parks is free of charge. Surrounded as it is today by a bustling city with a lot of traffic, there is still a peaceful air once inside the grounds.

The house was certainly full of mystery and surprise. One room contained a cupboard with mirrored panels, but when the door was opened, it wasn't a cupboard at all but three steps leading to another door that opened into a different room. This new room was lined with cupboards also, most of which were partitioned. However, one cupboard door led into a secret room that in turn had a secret catch in a cupboard in a different room that lifted one of the floorboards in this secret room. A further lattice door led to what might be called a safe room today, but it could have been a priest-hole when the house was built. The walls of the house were so thick that there were double doors, not side-by-side but on either side of the wall, and this meant there were extra deep hiding places for the children. There was a secret door behind one of the shelves of books in the library too, but to the children's disappointment, this was a fake door that didn't lead anywhere. There were impressive views from every window:

> The views from the windows were very beautiful; not a house was in sight anywhere. From the dining room, drawing-room, and library you looked across a downward slope of lawn and field on to the cool shining waters of the pool, from which the eye rose again up a green hillside to the thick belt of trees fringing the top of the hill. Above all soared the spire of St. Ann's Church.
>
> (*Richard Cadbury of Birmingham*)

Helen remembered how her father created an album, or scrapbook, all about Moseley Hall, filling it with old prints and photographs of both the hall and the village, along with newspaper cuttings and other notes. The new home, set in 22 acres, large and rambling, seemed like a magical land to the children:

> The garden of the house in Harborne Road with the adjoining garden of their grandfather, had always been a joy to the whole family, but the large estate surrounding Moseley Hall – with its fields and large pool, the tree-shaded island and adjoining bluebell woods, seemed almost like fairyland. The only sign of the nearby village was the spire of St. Ann's Church on Park Hill above the trees.
>
> (*Emma Richard Cadbury: 1846 – 1907*)

It even had extensive attics where the children could play or put on dramatic performances. Helen and Daisy had their own room up here, and there was a screaming room, where the children could run around and scream at the tops of their voices. The grounds were huge. There was a walled kitchen garden, a fig tree, fields, lawns, and a large copper beech where the young Beatrice imagined Alice's white rabbit must have disappeared down his hole in her adventures in Wonderland. On Good Friday mornings, this tree would also bear a very strange fruit – hot cross buns! Sometimes the buns would sprout on other trees around the garden too, so that the children had to hunt for them.

Barrow wrote:

> *One amusing little incident which occurred every Good Friday was the placing of hot-cross buns upon the trees in the gardens. We children used to look at the buds the day before. Needless to say that the time came when we discovered the way in which they grew, but the gathering was none the less a pleasure as we went out with our baskets.*
>
> *(Barrow Cadbury)*

The grounds surrounding the home included a bluebell wood and rabbits were often seen scampering around the garden. This led to the children calling the hall the bunny house. There were the family dogs and ponies too:

> *It was a fairytale home, and made all the sweeter by the addition of two family dogs: Duke, a retriever and Barry, a St Bernard puppy whom Beatrice adored. For her fourth birthday she was bought her very own Shetland pony, Dolly. Up until then she had ridden her nursery rocking horse, Dapple Grey, but her excitement knew no bounds when she sat upon Dolly's back and paraded proudly around the grounds, led carefully along by her nursemaid, Emma Denham.*
>
> *(Beatrice: The Cadbury Heiress Who Gave Away Her Fortune)*

There was a boathouse on the pool, and a flat-bottomed punt that held about fifteen people. The boys would run down and swim in the pool while the girls would push out the punt and linger beneath a tree to read or enjoy a picnic. The pool was well stocked and anglers were permitted to come and fish. William Cadbury recollected skating on the pool in the cold winters of the 1880s, but Helen's memories were clearer:

> *In winter it was the centre of outdoor attraction, and the skating, of which there was plenty during those years, was a never-to-be-forgotten joy. It was the only large sheet of ice in the neighbourhood, so in frosty weather it was thrown open to the public for a small entrance-fee, which was given to the funds of the Gospel Temperance Mission. What fun it was, when lessons were done, or the day's work ended, to rush down from the old Hall and join with the merry crowd on the ice! To think of it conjures back the ringing music of the skates, the nip of the frosty air, the bumps and collisions, the laughter and fun. How peaceful and refreshing it was in the quiet of early morning to skim over the shining surface, coming up to the house for breakfast with a healthy appetite; or at night, when the crowd had melted away, leaving perhaps a party of invited relations and friends, to glide to and fro by the light of the moon, or flaring torches stuck into the piles of snow, or Chinese lanterns held aloft, which seemed in the darkness to be moving like will-o'-the-wisps on the surface of the ice.*
>
> (*Richard Cadbury of Birmingham*)

And it wasn't just during the winter that the grounds came to life. In the spring there were snowdrops, violets, wood anemones, bluebells, and the pool glimmered azure, glinting in the sunlight. In the summertime the woods came alive. Richard's biggest delight was being able to share all of this natural beauty with others. The children gathered the flowers in baskets and walked into the village to give the flowers away to anyone who wanted them. When the bluebells were almost over, Richard would invite children from the slums to come and dash through the woods, to run and play, to shout and scream. In the mornings before breakfast, Richard would go out into the woods with an axe and cut away the dead wood. He cut down the elder trees too, which he called enemies because they choked the growth of other plants and shrubs. Sometimes he would spend this time teaching the children how to play tennis and sometimes he would pull dandelions out of the lawn.

Beatrice was born here in the spring of 1884, the last of Richard and Emma's children. And in the August of 1884, Richard Cadbury celebrated his fiftieth birthday, and a family party was held:

> *A large iced cake appeared on the table, with the name and the date in pink sugar, and as fifty candles were too many to go round it, a separate board was made, like a circular "Step Pyramid," and blazed in glory on a pedestal of its own. [...] the memory of the strong family affection which lay beneath it all is one of the deepest and sweetest things in life.*
>
> (*Richard Cadbury of Birmingham*)

Beatrice could remember happy Sunday evenings spent at home with their mother reading to them. A favourite book was *Sacred Allegories*. She also remembered the family singing hymns from the *Moody and Sankey Hymn Book*. The older children were mostly away at school. Jessie went to Edgbaston High School for Girls at first but moved to the Friends' boarding school in York, The Mount. Richard Jr had followed his older brother Barrow's example and spent some time in Stuttgart with Frau Kölle, while William studied engineering before joining the Sollwerk family, also in Germany. The Sollwerks were well-known manufacturers of cocoa and chocolate. When she was 9, Edith was sent to school in Weston-super-Mare for the sea air, as her health was not good. Richard was a good and loving father to all of his children, and while he could be strict when necessary, it wasn't something that sat naturally with him:

> *His love of children we can all speak of and his great tenderness in correcting them. When severe punishment was necessary I have known his eyes to stream with tears and he felt it probably much more than we did. His appearance year by year as Father Christmas was a continual joy to his children when young and his grandchildren in their turn. His fairy tales and stories were delightful. He would*

take an old scrapbook and weave around some picture the
most delightful story which for ever after made the picture
exceedingly real.

(*Barrow Cadbury*)

Emma Cadbury owned a phaeton, an open carriage pulled by just one horse. On Monday afternoons she would take her phaeton to her weekly mothers' meetings. The mothers' meeting in Bournville was attended by women who were connected to the firm in some way but couldn't get to church or meetings on a Sunday as they were at home cooking the dinner. Their children were also welcome and taken care of while the women enjoyed a quiet hour of religious contemplation. The family also had a closed carriage, in which they would often ride to visit John Cadbury in Harborne Road and George Cadbury, Richard's brother, at Woodbrooke in Selly Oak. In 1903, George was to found the only Quaker study centre in Europe in this home on the Bristol Road, where it is still in operation today.

In 1887, Richard's sister-in-law, George's wife, died, leaving his brother with three boys and two girls. When Jessie returned home from a visit to America soon afterwards, Richard sent her to help his brother care for the children.

Although Richard tried to keep business worries away from his home life, he didn't entirely shut everyone out. The house and grounds of Moseley Hall were often thrown open to those whose lives Richard touched and guests from the Sunday schools, from the adult classes, from the mothers' meetings and from the religious societies were all welcome. Larger parties were held out in the grounds and on the fields, with marquees erected in case of rain. Smaller parties were held within the house itself and in the smaller gardens. Every summer a temperance demonstration was held in the meadows that circled the grounds, with sometimes 20,000 – 30,000 visitors streaming in through the driveways. Refreshment tents were provided and, of course, no one ever got drunk. Other open-air meetings were held there, with Richard sometimes taking part himself and his children carrying around huge urns of hot tea as soon as they were big enough. The children would also play with the visiting children and even look after some of the babies.

Before the family moved out of Moseley Hall, Barrow married Geraldine Southall and went to live in Edgbaston, and Richard Jr had already gone to Adelaide to learn fruit-farming. John Cadbury would die on 11 May 1889, while the family still lived here. Richard's sister Maria finally married Joseph Fairfax and they went to live in Boulogne. The wedding turned out to be the last festivity held at the hall.

Beatrice remembered fondly her first seven years at Moseley Hall, but shortly afterwards, Richard gave the hall to the City of Birmingham for use as a children's convalescence home and the surrounding parkland to the town. Today it is a National Health Service (NHS) Community Hospital.

Uffculme

Richard and Emma had thought about donating Moseley Hall as a convalescent home for some time. They were concerned about how long it was taking the children of Birmingham to recover from their illnesses. They were convinced the children would recover much more quickly away from the factories and chimneys of the city – Birmingham was designated city status in 1889 – and that fresh country air and pleasant surroundings were much healthier. Moseley Hall seemed to be the ideal solution. Also, Richard had harboured dreams of building his own house to his own specification, and now he could afford it. For the first time in his life he would spend some of his money on himself.

Richard bought some land not far from Moseley Hall and built a new house named Uffculme, after the Devonshire village in which the Cadbury family ancestors had been sheltered. In November 1891, the family moved into their new home. The house was still close to Moseley Hall, and in fact the old hall could still be seen across the fields, but it had none of the trees. Instead it stood on open, sloping land: ...*which seemed to me* [Beatrice] *so open and bare, after the tall sheltering elms, with the rookery, around the old Hall.* (*Emma Richard Cadbury: 1846 – 1907*)

The house was built to a design of Richard's, which he had roughly sketched. The grounds were next to Highbury, which was politician Joseph Chamberlain's house. The lawns sloped past a couple of ponds and several fields, and led into Kings Heath Station down some wooden steps, whilst the other side of the grounds was flat. The Lickey Hills could be seen in the distance from the house, which was situated on the boundary between Kings Heath and Moseley. The Queensbridge Road separated the house from some larger fields: *These fields were used for summer parties for the many centres of mission and temperance work in the city. Open tea-sheds were built and proved a great convenience for the preparation of meals. (Emma Richard Cadbury: 1846 – 1907)*

Until recently there hadn't even been a road between the house and the fields, but instead just a footpath. Richard built a wall alongside the property, which turned out to block off the public view of the distant Lickey Hills. To compensate for this, he planted trees along the road instead, so that the locals could still enjoy a shady walk.

The first room to greet visitors to the new house was a great banqueting-type hall that took up the entire centre of the house, from front to back and from the floor to the roof. It was fitted out like a luxurious museum and contained, among other things, cases of stuffed birds, pinned butterflies, a stuffed emu next to the door to the library, a stuffed grizzly bear reclining on a settee, and antique furniture. Souvenirs and artefacts from Richard's travels filled every space. There was a vast fireplace with chairs to either side and a grand staircase leading off. Beatrice said that she hated it and Barrow thought it looked like some dour, dull, stuffy museum. Helen, however, gave the impression that all of the children loved the new house as much as their father did. The children *did* enjoy pretending to feed the emu and they had fun riding on the back of the bear, sometimes three at a time. A double-height conservatory held 10-foot palm trees, and a cockatoo called Cockey Boy lived in here along with some goldfish in a pool.

Another house, The Bunkoms, formed part of the estate, but was still occupied at the time Uffculme was completed. When The Bunkoms was vacated, the property was joined to Uffculme and pulled down, apart from two rooms, one of which was turned into a gym. There were woods at the back of this property where William later built a log cabin with his brother Barrow. Uffculme already had a short driveway leading from Queensbridge Road, but the addition of this property with its longer tree- and field-lined drive gave the home a second entrance.

The gardens were still the domain of Richard Cadbury, despite the family engaging several gardeners. He over-saw all of the work, in particular the ferns and rockeries, and he instructed that a marshy area be converted into a couple of ponds. These two pools were at different levels and were joined by a pretty little bridge. Instead of tents and marquees for the many gatherings, a tea shed was built in this garden. From the very first summer, the grounds at Uffculme were continually used for parties and get-togethers.

In 1890, Emma Cadbury's brother, William Wilson, and his wife had returned from Madagascar with their three children in tow: two girls and a boy. The boy was only 4 months old at the time. Four years later, when the Wilsons returned to Madagascar, they decided to leave the children in England to be educated. Richard and Emma took 4-year-old Alec into their own home and he was brought up alongside Beatrice, who adored having a little cousin to play with. Meanwhile, in 1892 and 1895, Barrow and Geraldine Cadbury had also been blessed with children, Dorothy (Dolly) and Paul, and so Richard became a grandfather. It never mattered how busy he was, he adored having all of the children around him. Even if he was working, if the children came into the library where he was writing, Richard would immediately down tools and gather them into his arms before planting them on the carpet with a picture book each.

On Sunday afternoons, big brother William would often invite the younger children to his room for tea and ginger biscuits whilst he read to them. Helen followed big sister Jessie to Edgbaston High School for Girls, Daisy went to boarding school in Darlington, and Beatrice was a pupil at the very first nursery school in Birmingham, in Harborne. The newcomer to the household, Alec, who had arrived at the home at the age of 4, also went to the nursery school, but when he was old enough he went to the boys' school on the corner of Hagley Road and Harborne Road at Five Ways. Beatrice remembered the dense fog that used to creep across the road and Cannon Hill Park, and she remembered that Alec had to be wrapped up against this fog because of poor health. Alec was given a small bedroom next to the nanny's room.

At 7.30 am every day, the entire household at Uffculme gathered for the morning reading, then after breakfast, Richard would make his way to the factory. He'd walk down to Dogpool Lane, where he would meet and jump on the mail van, or what he called his chariot. He liked to be at work early enough to lead the morning readings there. Surprisingly, at home the children had little chocolate, so it was always a treat on bank holidays for them to accompany their mother to the works and fill an empty box each with chocolates. Every Thursday afternoon, Emma would host an 'at home' day in the drawing room, where a grand piano stood along with a large Louis XIV clock.

The years 1896 and 1897 brought engagements for Jessie and Edith, with the first wedding taking place in April 1896 between Jessie and the Reverend T.G. Clarke. Just over a year later, at their home in Corby, Northamptonshire, their first child was born. A few months after the family returned from their 1897 travels, Edith was married at the meeting house in Bull Street and she and her husband, Arnold Butler, went to live at the house in Wheeley's Road, where she had been born. The meeting house was split into two sides, with the men and the boys sitting down one side, and the women and the girls on the other. Meanwhile, Richard, the youngest son, was in South Africa working a piece of land his father had bought for him in Cape Colony.

At around this time, Helen Cadbury was having a bit of a crisis of faith and she travelled to Germany to learn the language and study the music. While she was there she wanted to throw herself into the music and she wanted to go to the theatre. But she didn't want to defy her parents' beliefs without at least first telling them, although she had been convinced her musical education would not be complete without such a visit. And so she sought her parents' blessings for at least some of the operas. Richard wrote back to her from Wynds Point in Malvern:

> *Sunday, February 6th, 1898. – We have been spending a quiet day or two here, mother and I. It has been delightful weather, the sun shining brilliantly nearly all day. We have just been singing hymns together in the drawing-room. Mother has told me of thy chat with her about operas, and I promised to write to thee about it. Of course, thou are of an age to judge for thyself on such matters, and neither mother nor I wish to dictate or lay down our will against thy well-considered judgement. Nor do I know sufficient of the character and surroundings of such entertainments to go into any detail. I have been very happy without anything of the kind, and so far our dear children have not only had happy lives, but lives which have been untainted with the fascination that often draws young girls into worldly life and associations. I want thee to feel that we both have every confidence in thee, and are quite sure that thou wilt not enter into anything that thou knows thou cannot*

ask God's blessing upon. This is our safeguard, if we are honest to our convictions and make God's written word our rule of conduct. I have been reading a lovely little bit from J.J. Gurney, where he speaks of conscience as "sitting in the court of every man's soul as a judge." When truly guided by the Holy Spirit, it is the representative of God in our bosoms, and ought to reign supreme over all our actions, bodily and mental; and then he goes on to show how we may dethrone Conscience from her throne of "power" by our own wilfulness, although "the divine decree which establishes her authority" is still in force. I think we realise thy reasons on the question of the opera as the means of hearing musical talent, and of eduction [sic], and do not for a moment dispute it. Make it a matter of earnest prayer, and God will guide thee aright, and rest assured that we shall not judge thee. May the Lord bless thee, my darling, with His richest blessings, and make thee still a blessing to others. With dearest love from us all,

Thy affectionate father.

It seems from Helen's own words in her biography of her father that though she respected his wishes, she did in fact visit the theatre while she was abroad for a year studying, but she refrained from doing so when she was at home in Birmingham. The fact that Richard did not rant and rave and explicitly forbid her from doing as she wished, as per his own very strong religious beliefs, is a testament to the man's strength of character.

In 1896 and 1897, Richard wrote to two of his children on the occasions of their birthdays. Daisy was 18, and William would have been 30:

[To Daisy] *This is only a little note to send thee my dear love and good wishes on thy birthday. How quickly eighteen years have slipped away! It makes me feel quite old to have you all growing up into women. Well, it is after all but a little space to the end, but God has given us a better hope of the glorious land, where no sorrow or temptation shall come.*

Of course, it is not intended that we should be always thinking about that, but it is such a perfect rest to know that all is well with us, and with all we so dearly love.

[To William] *I wish especially to join with the others in wishing thee a very happy birthday, and that thy life may be spared for many a year, both for thy own blessing and for the happiness of all whom thou may influence for good. This indeed makes life worth living, and God has given us so many opportunities for making those around us happy that it becomes a duty as well as a privilege to do what we can, and this includes the little opportunities quite as much as the greater. I often have my heart full of praise to God that He has given my dear children this spirit. The Nile journey has been a great rest and enjoyment to me and to us all, and now I long to be at home again with you.*

When they moved into Uffculme, Richard and Emma had been married for twenty years. Five years later, in 1896, employee Tom Hackett was to recall the entire workforce being invited to Uffculme to celebrate another special day with the family:

One of the "Red Letter" days for Bournville was the occasion of the Silver Wedding party given by Mr. & Mrs. Richard Cadbury. The whole of the workpeople and their wives were invited to Uffculme, and on entering the grounds we were turned by our hosts in the Current [sic] and Raspberry Bushes (which contained a magnificent amount of fruit) and were told to help ourselves.

(A History of Cadbury)

Helen wrote, in 1906:

On July 20th the grounds of Uffculme were crowded with more than 2000 of the employees of Bournville, who had been given a holiday in honour of the event. Two days later a garden-party was given for relatives and members of the Society of Friends and on Saturday July 25th, the actual

*wedding day, about 930 men and women scholars of
class XV from Highgate, my father's adult school class,
took their turn in the festivities.*

*Urged by their children the bride and bridegroom
consented to go to Malvern for a miniature honeymoon.
The girls had insisted that their mother should have a
go-away dress, and a beautiful home-made bouquet and
buttonhole were provided. Maria Fairfax and Alice Wilson,
two of the bridesmaids of long ago, entered into the fun and
waited on the bride.*

(*Richard Cadbury of Birmingham*)

The happy couple had agreed to go on a miniature honeymoon because
Richard Cadbury had not wanted to miss his adult class on the day
following their actual anniversary. Their daughters had decorated
their four-wheeled carriage, the landau, and the horses with flowers
and foliage. And they tied an old shoe to the back of the carriage. By
now, Richard and Emma Jane were, of course, grandparents. Yet Emma
still looked beautiful in a floor-length brocade gown with puffed sleeves
and a tiny waist. Richard was 61, his hair was silver, his beard snow-
white. The day after they returned from this short break, they were
greeted by 3,200 women from the mothers' meetings of the Gospel
Temperance Mission.

In 1894, Richard and Emma Cadbury and their home at Uffculme
featured in *The Moseley Society Journal, Vol 1, No 5*, the opening of
which gives an insight into the character of Richard Cadbury:

*Illustrated Interviews. No. 1. MR. AND MRS. RICHARD
CADBURY AT UFFCULME*

*I need scarcely inform my readers that Mr. Richard
Cadbury is an exceptionally busy man. In addition to
the duties which his connection with the huge works at
Bournville involve, he is a philanthropist of the* working
*order, and devotes the whole of his time not occupied by
commercial duties to the furtherance of his many benevolent
projects. Consequently, the utmost difficulty is experienced
in gaining the smallest portion of his time, much less an
interview, which I was bold enough to plunge for. He is a*

man of most modest disposition, with a rooted objection to talking about himself, or his work. A considerable amount of encouragement and persuasion was needed, therefore, before my object was attained – in fact, had I not had the help of Mrs. Cadbury, I doubt if this interview would have seen the light, and certainly not in so complete a form. I could, and would have liked to, have given a lengthy review of the numerous good works and deeds for which Mr. Cadbury is responsible, but I am forbidden. All being precluded with the exception of those institutions, the public mention of which may prove beneficial to their future welfare and prosperity. Mr. Cadbury may be said to have inherited his great love for doing good and assisting those in distress, he being descended from a family which for generations has devoted both time and money to endeavouring to relieve suffering and elevate the masses. Both his father and grandfather were active workers in the Society of Friends, a body which has in itself been of immense service in leading the way in a quiet but sure and practical manner in all social reforms throughout the country, and especially in Birmingham.

This cutting, as well as others, can be found in the family book.

The family book

It was Richard who compiled all of the family's historical documents into what became known as *The Family Book*. This book was a record of the Cadbury family and their history with many additions collected by Richard himself. In fact, he would travel to Devonshire, where the family originated, to gather more research for this family tome.

The original Cadbury family were yeoman or tenant farmers when they lived in the West Country. Quakers were often persecuted or even imprisoned by the authorities and once it became clear that they were practising their religion, the families were turfed out of their farms and left to fend for themselves. Richard Cadbury would often travel to Devonshire to see where his ancestors once lived and worked, and he would sketch and paint pictures of the houses and farms. Samples of these sketches are included in the family book. Richard's first such excursion into the Devonshire family history occurred during the spring of 1861, which was the year he married Elizabeth Adlington and also the year he and his brother took control of the factory in Bridge Street. It was a busy year for him. On these visits, he searched for details of his ancestors and started to put them together into this family book in 1863.

During the Christmas holidays of 1848/49, the Birmingham Friends' Reading Society held their inaugural meeting. John Cadbury was the first president of the society and he arranged to have the meeting at the works in Bridge Street. The next few meetings were also held at Bridge Street, and Richard recorded some of the occasions in the family book:

The rooms were decorated with evergreens, and there were many interesting collections of curiosities and pictures displayed, which were lent by Friends for the amusement of the evening. After an address from the President, the rest of the business was condensed as much as possible, so that it might be a time of social intercourse and recreation. Part of the evening was spent in scientific experiments, such as the electric light, which was invented about that time. There were also readings of poetry and original papers. White and Pike had a printing press in the room some of the evenings, and printed cards in commemoration.

In the spring of 1866, Edward Cadbury, Richard's youngest brother, died. Richard remembered him in the family book:

He generally had great command over his temper, but once one of the younger boys had been taunting him with something that aroused his anger. He was about to strike the boy a heavy blow, when a man working on the premises was just in time to give Edward a push that knocked him over. He immediately got up, shook the man's hand, and thanked him for having been the means of stopping him in a moment's anger.

Only a few weeks later, John Cadbury, the oldest brother, took ill in Australia and was never to recover. Again, Richard added to the family book:

> *His letters show an earnest desire to alleviate the sufferings of those around him. He was almost over-sensitive of the levity and wickedness that his business brought him in contact with. In a letter written a few weeks before his decease, he mentions the case of a young man who lodged with him and who drank freely and went out rowing on the Sabbath. He had often spoken to him of the danger and wickedness of giving way to such practices, urging him to discontinue them, but without any lasting result; the end being that he was drowned in one of his Sabbath trips. On February 5th, 1866, he wrote: "We have just decided upon the building of our Meeting House, the ground and fencing all paid for. It will be capable of seating about fifty comfortably, and we may hope that when completed there may be real worshippers, not in the* form *but in the life, to offer up their hearts and wills to the teaching of our Heavenly Shepherd." John revelled in quiet country life, and his letters are full of allusions to nature's charms.*

The book currently resides in the library at Friends House in London, where it can be viewed by appointment. It's a massive scrapbook packed with newspaper cuttings, handwritten letters, and the various family trees of different branches of the family in Richard's own hand. On the front of the book is the legend *The Cadbury Pedigree*, and this is what the resource is known as at the library. The book contains pretty much most of what was known about the Cadbury family at the time of Richard's death.

Chapter 7

A creative life

Richard had a restful temperament. He was very creative and turned out to be very good at drawing and painting. He had inherited his father's eye for attractive detail and was a draughtsman who would often express himself in watercolour paintings. Richard also wrote poetry and verse, much of it religious in content. Natural history, geology and genealogy were other favourite topics for him. From the late 1860s, he designed many of the illustrations for Cadbury packaging.

In her book, *Cadbury's Angels*, Iris Carrington (granddaughter of Richard's brother George, so therefore his great-niece) wrote:

> *United as they were by a shared Quaker philosophy, the brothers naturally differed in many ways. Richard was quiet and not particularly ambitious. He would perhaps have been content to rescue the business, and see it prosper on a small scale. He had an artistic temperament, with sufficient skill to produce commercial illustrations for the business. He also wrote poetry, chiefly of a religious character, and was devoted to 'good works', in the family traditions.*
>
> *(Cadbury's Angels)*

From a very young age Richard displayed this artistic streak, and there were portfolios filled with examples of his paintings and drawings of landscapes, figures, trees and flowers. He would hang a large sheet of paper on the wall and take a stick of charcoal to quickly sketch a mountain scene. Many of his watercolours were given to his wife as gifts, and they adorned her bedroom walls.

Despite their differences, the brothers shared the same ideas and work ethic. Richard had started to make pictorial designs that could be used on the lids of chocolate boxes and had them printed in sheets. It was he who came up with the idea of replacing plain labels with attractive pictures, but when he looked around, he couldn't find enough designs that he liked. Instead he started to design them himself, doing the paintings in his free evenings at home. The first such label was printed in 1868 and depicted a little girl in a muslin frock, with a red flower in her hair, who was holding a kitten upon her lap. The picture was used on boxes of chocolate crèmes from 1869. Another early picture was used on the cover of *Cadbury's Angels* by Iris Carrington.

Richard used his own children as models for his early paintings and scenic views were inspired by family holidays to Switzerland. Many of his designs can be seen today in the family book, at Friends House in London, where it is known as *The Cadbury Pedigree*.

A portrait of Richard's mother, Candia, who died in 1855, hung on the wall of Richard's dressing room, surrounded by pictures of his three late brothers, John, Edward and Henry. On the back of his mother's picture was a poem written in his own hand:

> *MY MOTHER*
> *From gentle bowers among the flowers*
> *The sweetest perfumes rise;*
> *My mother's love thus gilds the hours*
> *Of memory's changing skies.*
>
> *Our childhood's day has passed away,*
> *Yet not our childhood's dream;*
> *The vista of its chequered way*
> *Is like a silver stream.*
>
> *Can Heaven bestow a warmer glow*
> *Of sunshine from above;*
> *A purer, holier pledge below*
> *Than in a mother's love?*
>
> (Richard Cadbury of Birmingham)

Much of Richard's poetry was religious in content, but he could also be amusing. When the brothers took control of the firm of Cadbury, the product was considered of an inferior quality (see Chapter 4), and George Cadbury in particular gave evidence to a committee appointed to consider the Adulteration of Food Act of 1872. By 1866, the company had launched its own higher quality Cocoa Essence, and it is possible, but not confirmed, that Richard may have come up with the following verse:

> *To adulterate Cocoa's become such a practice*
> *That really the State must step in to protect us,*
> *The faculty tell us to drink, but the fact is*
> *The stuff is so starched they can hardly expect us.*
> *Who wish for pure cocoa in all its quintessence*
> *Will certainly find it in Cadbury's Essence.*
> > *(The Firm of Cadbury: 1831 – 1931)*

In the summer of 1860, four of the American cousins came over for a visit on their way to the continent. Much of the English family gathered at Richard Tapper Cadbury's home on 16 August to greet them. Richard Barrow Cadbury designed a greeting card to be given to each person present as a small memento of the event. The card depicted a floral spray encircled with a wreath of olive leaves and fruit and surrounded by a bundle of sticks. The motto *Felices ter et amplius quos irrupta tenet copula*, which roughly translates as 'thrice blessed are those who enjoy uninterrupted union, and more' (Google Translate), was also on the card, and a couple of verses composed by Richard were within:

> *Thrice happy they whom love entwines in memory's wreath*
> > *together,*
> *'Tis better far when joy combines than any earthly treasure;*
> *Columbia's star shall brighter glow, and Albion fairer seem,*
> *Now that our kindred feelings flow in one unbroken stream.*
>
> *Heaven's choicest gifts blend all in one, as dew-drops in a*
> > *flower,*
> *Or as when streamlets meeting run in union each bright*
> > *hour;*
> *So may the olive round us be an evergreen of love,*
> *And may each branch or parent tree unite in Heaven above.*
> > *(Richard Cadbury of Birmingham)*

On 26 February 1879, Richard's Uncle Barrow and Aunt Candia celebrated their golden wedding anniversary. In celebration of the event, Richard wrote a poem:

Full fifty years have passed away
Since two young hearts were light and gay;
And each in confidence confessed
The love that fluttered in the breast.

And now a sweeter, holier flame
Binds earth to heaven in higher aim;
Whose souls thus linked in earthly bliss
Long for eternal happiness.

Sweet memories linger on the years
That time has oft bedewed with tears;
Tears that reflect the sunlit rays
From Him who filled their hearts with praise.

A daily providence we trace
In mercies shed with boundless grace;
Each year God's sheaves of golden grain
Have blessed the hours of toil and pain.

And now with garnered sheaves they stand
Like pilgrims near the promised land,
With willing hearts to lay them down,
For heaven's sure, untarnished crown.

Richard wrote his wife Emma a letter on 26 February 1880, enclosing a newspaper cutting he had clipped out. He was delighting at fatherhood, and saying how much he was missing Daisy (Margaret). The letter also included the following lines of verse:

Patter, patter, little feet,
In the room above my head;
Not a sound is half so sweet,
There is music in their tread.

Happily they trip along,
Airy, fairy, light, and gay,
Keeping time to an old song,
Bringing back a bygone day.

As I listen to the sound,
What a vision greets my eye
Just a wee thing toddling round,
With its mother standing by.
Love is light upon her face
With a beauty most divine;
Over all the crowning grace, –
Child and mother both are mine.

Richard was such a poet that his daughter Helen published a short book containing some examples. The following are a mix of some of those examples and some that were found among a series of essays Richard also wrote. Where the dates the poems were written are known, they are included:

The Homeland (1857)
Home, home, we are out on the tack
For the land so brave and free,
Where the happiest faces greet us back –
'Tis the fairest land to me.

I'll seek not you, ye raging waves,
Ye waters of the sea;
For there's not a land that Nature's spared
So many gifts as thee.

God's Messengers (unknown)
I passed a wretched labyrinth of homes,
Where the sweet woodland zephyr never comes,
Nor rose nor woodbine grow with perfume rare,
But smoke and close infection taint the air.

High from the loud and angry cloud below,
A garret window caught a sunny glow;

93

Oh! how like hope this gleam of light may be!
Dispersing clouds and setting sad hearts free!

A little maiden clasped her hands in prayer,
Seeking in faith and hope God's presence there,
And asking for His holy land to stay
The curse, that led her dearest ones astray.

Great God, Thou knowest all that dwells within;
Wilt Thou, who art too pure to look on sin,
Be with a trembling heart, amid this shade,
And listen to a little one who asks Thy aid?

Rest, helpless, weary one! in patience, rest!
The battle is the Lord's; His will is best:
For He can reign who rules the stormy sea,
And still the tempter's power, and care for thee.

God answers all who humbly rest in Him,
And though the night be long, and hope be dim,
Morn ushers angels in with radiant wings
To bear thy sorrow to the King of kings.

Sweetly reposing, in God's love abide,
Calm as a placid lake at eventide;
Reflecting visions of the heaven above,
And walking in that realm where all is love.

Then shall we not, as little children, pray
That we may be God's messenger to-day;
For what we do and what we say may be
God's beacon-light to set some captive free.

Spring (unknown)
Beautiful springtime, we welcome thy coming;
The dark days of winter are passing away;
In mossy banks, flowerets their bright heads are showing,
And feathered tribes carol thy steps with their lay.

A CREATIVE LIFE

We welcome thy coming, sweet charmer of nature,
In embryo waiting thy warm, genial showers,
To unfold the leaf with the soft breathing zephyr,
And change the bare woodlands to garlands and bowers.

When early morn dawns on the eastern horizon,
A ruby light fringes the curtains of night,
Till the sun rises forth from the mist to emblazon
And o'er-spread the earth with his mantle of light.

Thus April invites with its soft rain and gleaming
Those fair-formed beauties in woodlands we love;
Each clothed in its glory of colouring – seeming
Like scattered tears dropped from the rainbow above.

A grassy lane passing through copses and moorland,
By cornfields and meadows, where troops of lambs play,
Charms our steps on to revel with Nature's wild garland,
In ferny nooks shaded by branches of may.

From each pendant twig is a lustrous gem hanging;
The breath of the morning, distilled into dew,
Which from its white blossoms sweet odour is bringing
To mingle with that of the violet blue.   .

Hard by, in the valley, a rustic bridge crosses
A clear mountain stream that runs purling along,
Where a fair country maiden stands combing her tresses,
And blends her sweet voice with the thrushes' full song.

Her playmates have left her to search in the forest,
For flowers to wreathe with the red and white may,
And now return laden with garlands the choicest,
To crown her their May Queen in innocent play.

Thus waits the young springtime, festooned like the maiden,
The queen of the year in her virgin robes dressed,

For the sunshiny summer to cherish, who's laden
With fruits from the flowers her presence had blessed.

Angels (1869)
Children of heaven, the anthem you raise
On earth is a jubilant echo of praise;
Sweetly the strain falleth soft on the ear,
Angels are telling us Jesus is near;
Swiftly they break through the cloud and the gloom,
Shining as light from their glorious home;
Higher to beckon us, children of night,
Gladly to welcome us, children of light.

Welcome we give you, bright angels, below,
Silently striving to comfort our woe;
Angels of mercy watch over us here,
In sorrow or joy, sweet spirits, be near;
Come when in anguish and sooth us with calm,
Come when we joy most and shield us from harm;
Guardian Angels, we yearn for your love,
Foretaste of higher and purer above.

Angels of patience, with gladdening wings,
Bless every sorrow humanity brings;
Mother, why weepest thou? dry up thy tears,
Angels are waiting to banish thy fears,
Nought hast thou here when God calls thee away,
Seek thou for glories that never decay;
Seek the pearl gates that thy loved ones have found,
Thank Him that they have reached holier ground.

Pilgrim of earth, upon life's troubled sea,
The Angel of Hope thy best pilot will be;
Cast in thy anchor when calms would ensnare,
Press for the harbour when breezes are fair;
Fear not, but trust on His arm to rely,
Hope fills thy canvas, the land to descry;

Bring others with thee its glories to see,
Hearken, the angels are welcome thee.

The Angel's Song (1869)
My hymn is praise,
My song is love,
My home is with the blest above;
I joy to raise
My song to Thee
For all Thy gifts and love to me.

To Thee, my King,
Is glory due,
For ever let my song be new;
Oh let it ring
In cadence sweet
For ever where the spirits meet.

Around Thy throne
We pray to Thee,
That peace on all the earth may be;
For Thou wilt own
The sinner's sigh
And welcome to Thy courts on high.

Oh Lamb of God,
We angels bright
Would gather in the harvest white;
We kiss the rod
That makes us Thine,
So may Thy saints in glory shine.

Come and rejoice,
Rejoice with me
To welcome in a spirit free;
All in one voice
An anthem raise,
Of glory to our God and praise.

The following poem was one of several written in an album that were accompanied by original illustrations in watercolour:

The Daisy (1876)
There is a little flower I love
That drinks in sunshine from above,
Is watered by the dew,
Lies nestled in the moss and grass
And closes, when the dark nights pass,
Its eye of golden hue.

Its dainty petals, white as snow,
Are bidden from the winds that blow,
And fast to each embrace.
But early morn soon opens wide
The ruby lips that, watchful, bide
Its bonnie little face.

The welcome, little English flower,
I fain would offer as my dower
To thee is love's behest;
That thou wouldst flourish at my side,
And by thy sweetness banish pride
For ever from my breast.

Richard didn't confine his writing talents to poetry. He was also a member of the Friends' Essay Society, a Quaker institution that provided 'intellectual entertainment for social gatherings in place of the dancing and card-playing of other circles'. (*Richard Cadbury of Birmingham*) These essays were bound into volumes, and the first one of Richard's to appear was entitled *The Jews*. Interestingly, the last, written after his visit to Egypt in 1897, was entitled *The Jewish Race in Egypt*. Both demonstrate Richard's great 'knowledge of Hebrew and Egyptian history'. Other essays were entitled: *The influence of Early Education on After Life; Does the Cultivation of the Mental Faculties increase Temporal Happiness?*; *Ireland and her Wrongs*; and *Liberty*.

Other essays were on sleep, mercy, *Half an Hour in James Watts' Workshop, Cloisters of the Friars, The Roman Villa near Brading,* summer, and winter. Over the years these diverse topics showed their author's diverse interests and knowledge. Helen Cadbury Alexander included some extracts in her *Richard Cadbury of Birmingham*. These extracts are also included here to give an idea of Richard's writing style. From the essay entitled *Liberty* is the ending:

> Perfect *liberty is – and ever will be – like a far-off star; a beautiful world gilded in its own brilliancy; a Utopia impossible to obtain, except in imagination.*
>
> *It is like a delicate flower that, when grasped, is crushed in our embrace. Never will its untarnished beauty be realised in this world, but with victory over the sin that now stains its fair white petals it will be worn as an emblem of purity in paradise.*

From *Nature and Art*:

> *A prominent feature in nature is, that green constitutes the chief colour in those objects upon which we rest our sight, and is in its fullest perfection when we need it most. It is hardly necessary to be reminded of the pleasure there is when spring-time harbingers the light green leaf of grass and tree; and later when the sun is in his zenith, how delicious it is to wander under the darker shade of the forest. Green also forms the best contrast to bright colours; the charm that flowers have would be lost if they had not the fresh and cool background that it affords. The eye thirsts for it somewhat in the same way as the tongue for water, and it seems especially adapted to rest the optic nerves when the sight is over-strained. Green is eminently the colour which God has chosen for man, to invigorate his mind and refresh his body; and even those who live in large cities and who love the freshness of its natural charms may still apply it in the art of decoration.*
>
> *With gold it forms one of the prettiest finishes to interior decoration, while it adds coolness and cheerfulness to have the shutters and sunblinds or the prominent woodwork painted an emerald green. It forms at the same time a*

pleasant contrast to the dull reds and smoky browns that are all but universal.

We too often find a total disregard for this – nature's choicest colour – in the laying out of our suburban gardens. A border of box – or perhaps a row of tiles, surrounding a bed of gooseberry trees and cabbages is a work of [art?] *for the eye to rest on in dreary contemplation.*

Trelliswork produces an effect that represents in a stiff form the beautiful intertwining in nature, and whether it be placed against the wall or used as a verandah, it is a great relief to the broad face of bricks and mortar, and at once invites the opportunity for allowing nature also to do her share in its embellishment.

White is the emblem of purity, and not only the emblem but the test. As purity is essential to health, its introduction on this account is important; it is also indispensable as a contrast, and to give value to colour. The delicate tint of the skin is always enhanced by the contrast of white, and perhaps the loveliest picture we can look on is a beautiful woman dressed in pure white.

Whenever colour is introduced it should be bright and pure, to produce a pleasing effect, but never in too large masses or in too great variety. The better taste is that bright colour should be used only as a relief upon a subdued groundwork, because if the sight be arrested by a distinct and pure colour, the subdued background will remain in some measure undefined; and as a brilliant dash of colour in dress or in an apartment will give a life that it would not otherwise possess.

The mind becomes cramped by living too much among the works of our own creation; but nature will teach what cannot otherwise be learnt, in nobility and power, in grace and beauty. It is among the rugged mountains wrapped in grey mists, and on the wide ocean and desert, or in the quiet valley where flocks are grazing and the distant hills are bathed in hazy light, that we drink in and appropriate new ideas, which again and again come before us in the everyday business of life.

Chapter 8

Religion, the mission, and other philanthropy

Richard Cadbury was a great lover of children and hated to see any child suffer. Not long after the death of his first wife Elizabeth, Richard met the widow Mrs Wilson, who had been left with seven children of her own. With four young children himself, he was very grateful for the experience and advice of Mrs Wilson. His daughter Helen later wrote in her biography of him:

> *She [...] gladly gave her help and advice to her young acquaintance. The shadow of grief which had fallen upon his own life only served to deepen Richard Cadbury's natural thoughtfulness for others. [...] His passionate devotion to his own children, and his joy in fatherhood, was but a special phase of his great love to all children. One of the things which grieved his tender heart almost more than anything else was the sight of a child in pain or misery. He always longed that children should have a real child-life, and not be burdened before their time with care and responsibility. In walking to and from his home in Wheeley's Road to the factory in Bridge Street, he had to pass through a district which already had begun to be thickly populated. Day by day, as he walked through some of the back streets, he would notice the children playing in the gutters – little toddlers running about the roads in imminent danger of the traffic, and babies being dragged about and nursed by children hardly bigger than themselves. Often as he spoke of these things his eyes would fill with tears, and his voice would break, and as he played with his four little ones in*

their safe and sheltered home, his heart would go out to
the hundreds of neglected, uncared-for children in the city
streets.

(*Richard Cadbury of Birmingham*)

The more Richard thought about these poor children, the more the germ of an idea started to take root in the back of his mind. He had seen day nurseries on the continent on his many travels, so he knew a similar system could be adopted at home. In fact, he had spoken of the idea with his late wife and she had felt equally as strongly about the subject. Now he wanted to do something about it, in her memory and in memory of his own mother. If God had seen fit to allow Richard to prosper, the least Richard could do was give something back, or pay it forward.

He discussed the idea with his new friend Mrs Wilson, deciding to start small and, if successful, grow it into something much bigger. Helen continued:

He looked about for a house in a suitable position, and
succeeded in finding an empty corner-house in Bishopgate
Street, which he rented. He then commissioned his friend to
find a suitable matron, being anxious to make the scheme
helpful. A poor widow, with five children, who was in great
distress, was recommended for the position. Assured that
she was honest and sober, Richard Cadbury at once supplied
her immediate wants, rented the house, and set Mrs. Dyson
to clean it out thoroughly. [The distressed widow] *was full*
of gratitude and delight at thus being able to maintain her
independence. Having watched in this preliminary interval
to see how much real interest she had in the scheme, and
how she managed her own children and her home, Richard
Cadbury felt satisfied that he had found the right woman to
act as matron.

(*Richard Cadbury of Birmingham*)

On the first day there were five children at the day nursery, but soon after there were more. And still Richard was not content that he was doing enough to help them. He would often visit the homes of the children too, and Mrs Dyson would draw his attention to what she considered special cases. Even his own children accompanied him to both the nursery and the homes of the children, and they were encouraged to share their toys and games with those less privileged: *For weeks before a seaside holiday they would save up empty match-boxes, to be packed with shells for the children at the day nursery.' (Richard Cadbury of Birmingham*)

Being quite the creative handyman, Richard found pleasure in inventing contraptions that would help the children further. These included a large hanging cradle that was suspended from the ceiling. The cradle was big enough to hold several infants at once and would swing from side to side, rocking them to sleep. He also designed several different sizes of bench to suit the varying sizes of the children, as well as a series of playpens to keep those children just starting to toddle safe while they played. The children were introduced to hygiene too:

> *The babies were always bathed and kept beautifully clean. This cleanliness occasionally roused astonishment during the first months amongst the owners of the children. One day a girl, coming for her sister's baby, could not at first distinguish it from among the others; it was so changed from the dirty, ill-kempt little mortal that had been brought in the morning. At last she discovered it, and picked it up, exclaiming, "My! Yer own mother won't know yer!"*
> (*Richard Cadbury of Birmingham*)

A separate meeting was held on Wednesdays for the mothers of the children, overseen by Mrs Wilson. During these meetings, the women were taught how to apply Christianity in their homes, good home management, and total abstinence. On Sunday evenings another meeting was started that began at 8.00 pm. This time both parents of the children, if applicable, were invited. Richard liked to keep an eye on these meetings, and sometimes gave a gospel address to the Sunday evening attendees.

Only a few years after founding the day nursery, Richard Cadbury took the house next door to the original in Bishopgate Street and knocked them both into one. But now, with the organisation growing, Richard encouraged others to become involved and started a committee in November 1873. The first such annual committee meeting took place on 19 November, with proper minutes, reports, and so on.

Richard and his second wife Emma both came from religiously devout backgrounds, although Richard was, of course, a Quaker, and Emma was a member of the congregational church in Carrs Lane. Carrs Lane Church was originally built in the mid-1700s as a small chapel. It was extended twice, and given a new frontage in the early 1800s. It became part of the Congregational Union in 1832. A much more modern building stands on the spot today, built in 1971, and the congregational church was merged with the Presbyterian church to become part of the United Reformed Church.

Quakers were not expected to marry outside of the Quaker tradition, due to the risk of a dilution of belief. To Richard, the teaching and the practice of Christianity was important, so he concentrated on mission work as well as temperance. Emma resisted joining the Society of Friends for two years, but she still accompanied him to his meetings and he accompanied Emma to hers. However, in 1873, by her own volition, and despite her reservations (for example, she was always accustomed to the singing of hymns to accompany her own religion, yet there was no music during Friends' meetings and even some long silences), Emma decided to convert to her husband's faith. One of her brothers also became a Friend.

Mornings in the family home in Moseley Hall began at 7.30 am when Richard and Emma and all eight of Richard's children (when they were home) would gather. Following a Bible reading and a prayer, Richard would kiss each of his children and then his wife before setting off for work. The golden family age that began when they moved into Moseley Hall also spilt over into a golden age for the chocolate manufactory. As the business grew, so too did the Cadbury brothers' personal wealth. In order to reconcile this with their Quaker beliefs, both George and Richard Cadbury considered themselves to be custodians of this wealth and they felt it pertinent to share it with those more in need than themselves. They felt it was their responsibility to do some good where they could.

Adult classes

The parliamentary Bill that ensured compulsory elementary education for all was not passed until 1870. This meant that there were grown men and women all over the country who could not read and write. As far as the Quakers were concerned, this also meant they were unable to read and enjoy the Bible. Many weren't a part of any religious movement, so the Bible wasn't indoctrinated within them from an early age either.

It was during a conversation between members of the Society of Friends that the idea of classes for adults first cropped up. The discussion took place in Joseph Sturge's house in Wheeley's Road. In his *Life of George Cadbury*, A.G. Gardiner wrote of this new adult school movement:

> *The feeling found its expression through Joseph Sturge, a man of enlightened and public-spirited mind, whose name is associated in the annals of Birmingham with many admirable causes. The idea to which he gave form did not originate with him. It first took root in Nottingham as far back as 1798, when William Singleton and Samuel Fox opened a Sunday School for adults, in which reading and writing were taught as well as the Bible. This school, which still exists, was visited by Joseph Sturge in 1842, and he was so impressed by the practical and spiritual works that he considered the idea of introducing it to Birmingham. It was not, however, until 1845 that, with his brother, he found it convenient to make the experiment. It was at the Severn Street Schools that the movement was begun. The immediate purpose was educational. The school gathered together the illiterate dwellers of the slums in the early hours of Sunday morning, and provided them with instruction in the rudiments of learning. The proportion of illiterates in the working-class population of those days was very high, and remained high until the generation which was brought under the Education Act of 1870 grew up.*

Although classes had already been taking place in towns such as Bristol and Nottingham, Sturge and a few other Friends started Sunday evening classes for young men aged 14 and over in 1845. They were the first to take place in Birmingham. When attendance started to drop off during the summer months, the classes were moved to 7.30 am, and early morning schools caught on.

The main reason for these classes was to help stamp out illiteracy. Attendees learnt how to read and write using the Bible as a textbook. Richenda Scott wrote a biography of Elizabeth Cadbury and she is quoted in the biography of Barrow Cadbury:

> *George Cadbury, in 1859, had been drawn into the work of the Adult School which Joseph Sturge had opened at Severn Street. From 1863* [George] *was given charge of a class of men, Class XIV, with which his connection remained unbroken for fifty years. Every Sunday morning in all weathers it was his practice to ride into Severn Street on horseback to hold his class and to share in the breakfast provided for the teachers before the Adult School opened at 7.30 a.m.*
>
> (*Elizabeth Cadbury*)

Richard occasionally taught the adult class in Severn Street himself on Sundays, or he was called upon to make a speech or give a talk. He was only 10 years old at the time of the first class but during his lifetime, the movement increased to thirty-eight different classes across Birmingham. The classes in Severn Street were broken into two parts, whereby one group learnt reading and writing while the other studied the scriptures in the first half of the session, and the other way around during the second half of the session. Richard's friend from his youth, J.W. Shorthouse, wrote: *Before he had a First Day school class of his own he often took mine when I was prevented, and he was much valued as a substitute by other teachers also.* (*Richard Cadbury of Birmingham*)

After their marriage in July 1871, Emma joined in with many of Richard's interests, one of which was to become the Adult School Movement, which had been started in 1845 by Joseph Sturge and his brother. Sturge was a Quaker and an anti-slavery campaigner. Elementary education was not made compulsory until 1870, and there were many men and women who could neither read or write. It started with a group of men who met with Joseph and his brother on a Sunday morning in a building in Severn Street. Using the Bible as their textbook, lessons started with a little speech from the organisers, perhaps a passage or two read from the Bible, or maybe a prayer before the meeting was broken up into smaller more manageable groups.

These classes weren't always appreciated by the local population. Indeed, when one class turned up in Selly Oak, there was dissent. A.G. Gardiner explained:

> *The effect of the movement in the Selly Oak district was very marked. It penetrated to the very lowest stratum of society, and brought within its influence large numbers of men who were outside the range of the organized churches. Drink and the jerry-builder* [builder of poorly built properties] *were the twin evils of the district, and those who profited by them were not slow to resent an invasion that threatened their empire. A strong spirit of antagonism towards the movement manifested itself. This was especially directed against George Cadbury and his brother. The establishment of their works near by at Bournville, and their practical enthusiasm for housing, was a challenge, the meaning of which the jerry-builder and the publican were not slow to understand. The advent of the Adult School marked a new phase of the attack, and there commenced a struggle between the two forces which continued for the best part of a generation. The attacks on the Cadburys generally took the form of worthless slander, but occasionally they were more direct.*
>
> (*Life of George Cadbury*)

In other words, the bosses who built the shoddy housing and the people who sold the cheap booze were not at all happy with these so-called do-gooders educating their workers and their clientele on good housing, education for all, and temperance. However, a more positive reflection has been reproduced in Appendix III.

The Highgate Mission

In 1876, a woman by the name of Mrs William Lloyd founded a day nursery and orphanage in a house in Montpellier Street, Balsall Heath. Here the homeless and those without parents were able to receive some care. This same house was used for various gospel and religious meetings as well, most notably the Severn Street Christian Society, which convened there on a Sunday evening. While members of other religious organisations were not encouraged to come along to these meetings, a branch committee of the Severn Street school was formed at the day nursery. Before long, the idea of an adult school here was floated, and three Bibles, a number of books and a school secretary were promised and appointed. In the 1880s, a hut was erected in Upper Highgate Street.

George Cadbury was a regular teacher at the Severn Street adult school, and Richard too started by teaching the men to write in a Bible and literacy class. In 1877, Class XIV moved from Severn Street to the Board School on Bristol Street. At the same time, the class grew and new classes grew up out of this one. When the satellite branch in Montpellier Street started to cast around for a potential teacher, the name Richard Cadbury sprang to mind.

Richard thought about the offer very carefully, and he agreed to take the position at least temporarily. He was, after all, already a very busy man with a large family and a family business to help look after, but still he became leader of the group in this corrugated iron mission room. In the end he continued teaching the classes until the end of his life. Whenever he was home, at 7.00 am on a Sunday morning he would head off to meet the other group leaders for breakfast, sometimes walking through deep snow to get there. In 1888, Richard wrote an account of the origin of Class XV, or what he called the Highgate Mission:

> *It was started in a small room at Montpellier Street, the entrance being in Kyrwick's Lane, near Camp Hill Station, through the garden of what used to be a very pleasant country house, used as a* crèche *by Mrs. William Lloyd. In the field at the back of the house a long, two-storied* [sic] *shed had been erected, the basement of which formed the room in question. The ceiling was very low, and the light and ventilation not of a superior character. In winter, a small gas-stove was the medium of warmth, and owing to the gas-pipes being near the surface of the ground, it was often the case that neither light nor warmth could be obtained.*
>
> [...] *Many initial difficulties had to be overcome, in the way of starting the various societies inseparable from*

school work, such as sick club, dispensary fund, savings'
fund, etc., and more than once in the depth of winter we
have sat together in our top-coats, with a tallow candle
as our only light. Many of our new scholars left under
the somewhat hard discipline, but, notwithstanding all
these difficulties, the room was well filled with about sixty
scholars during the summer months, and many a happy
hour was spent together.

We remember with gratitude the kindness and sympathy
of Mrs. Lloyd, who was always ready to help us in the work.
Meetings for worship were held on Sunday evenings in
the same rooms, conducted by the Severn Street Christian
Society, and these meetings much encouraged those who
had made a new start in life to continue in the right way.
In 1879 it was felt that no further development of the
class could be made in this room, so after much anxious
deliberation we agreed to make a move to the board schools
near Highgate Park.

(Richard Cadbury of Birmingham)

After he finished his training in London, in 1881 Barrow joined his
father at the mission and was given his own class at the junior school
in Chandos Road. After Class XV was moved to near to Highgate Park,
there was an increase in attendance and the class spread into the nearby
Moseley Road School. A new iron hut was rented in Upper Highgate
Street for meetings on week nights. One of the attendees remembered:

After a time we felt that there were too many good men with
nothing to do, so six of us went out one Sunday night in
May, about 1880, down to Queen Street, Sparkbrook, and
began to sing and carry on mission work. In September of
the same year Mr. Cadbury came down to see us, and we
said to him, "Well, sir, what are you going to do now that
we have a congregation?" Mr. Cadbury replied, "I will find
you a place." There was a man in Highgate with a little iron
hall. Mr. Cadbury went to see this man and rented the hall
from him. It held about seventy or eighty people, and he
told us that as soon as we filled it he would build a bigger.

Then we set to work to fill the place. We told Mr. Cadbury that we wanted some tracts; he got some immediately, and helped us get them ready for distribution. He was like the captain of a band of men, ready to work. The consequence was that we soon filled the hall.

(Richard Cadbury of Birmingham)

The iron room, as it came to be known, in Upper Highgate Street, was also used on a Sunday evening for meetings. In fact, it proved to be so useful that, in 1884, Richard bought it. By 1886, the old iron room was no longer adequate and the meetings moved to a new, open space on Conybere Street. After it was moved, it was used for one of the new Gospel Temperance women's meetings – to become known as the Gospel Temperance Mission. In the early 1880s, another hut was erected in Upper Highgate Street.

After classes had finished for the day, Emma and the children would join Richard at the meeting in Bull Street, where the men would sit on one side and the women the other. When Beatrice was born, Emma too became involved in what was to become the women's equivalent of this group, the mothers' meeting. When the children were older, they were expected to take their civic duties seriously as well.

In late spring, Beatrice and her nursemaid would pick bluebells from the field at Moseley Hall to make posies to distribute in the poorer areas of Birmingham. Emma Jane encouraged the girls to hold pin sales at home, with the 'proceeds' going to help underprivileged children. At Christmas time, the sisters would form their own mini-production line, grating suet, stoning raisins and washing currants to make Christmas puddings for families in need.

(Beatrice: The Cadbury Heiress Who Gave Away Her Fortune)

When children from the Birmingham slums started to make day trips to Moseley Hall, Richard sent his own children upstairs to raid their own closets and cupboards and give something to these poor children who didn't have any shoes or who had dirty and matted hair. He would order the cook to make them a vat of warm milk, to which he added cocoa.

His own girls would then serve the visiting children on the lawn outside, with a hot drink and a bun each.

Barrow was asked to go along to the school in Montpellier Street to teach writing. He said: *I wrote a clear hand, while there were thousands of men who could not write; and the power to read and write added to the richness of their lives. (Barrow Cadbury)* He also remembered that milk was regularly provided for the helpers on arrival at Severn Street at 7.30 am on Sundays as well as breakfast at 9.30 am after class had finished. Then the Friends would make the 3-mile walk into Birmingham in time for morning worship at the Friends' Meeting House in Bull Street.

The *Moody and Sankey Hymn Book* was often used at meetings, and Richard and Emma would frequently lead singing of the hymns at home, which differed considerably from the Anglican hymns of the same time. Apparently, the words and the melodies were different and the hymns had a different feel to them. The Quaker movement suffered a troubled period around the 1850s, both in England and America, and there was a split. The Hicksite Friends separated from the more orthodox Friends and in England, a strong evangelical revival opposed the Hicksites. Foreign missionary work was begun and the Friends' spirit soared, strengthened by the Moody and Sankey hymns. The new Upper Highgate Street mission was inspired by this newfound enthusiasm and centres sprung up across the city. One year, a week of tent missions was also held in each of the centres.

Richard Cadbury built the Moseley Road Institute in 1878 in order to bring together adult schools, Sunday schools and other associated mission work. After Richard's death in 1899, later that same year, Barrow Cadbury took on the mantle and continued to develop his late father's work.

Children's convalescence

For some time, Richard Cadbury was keen to find a location that would be suitable for convalescing children. Helen explained:

> *With the street as their only playground, the constant noise of the town dinning in their ears all day, and the stifling atmosphere of their often unsanitary homes, it was no*

wonder if the less robust boys and girls fell sick and pined
away, even when they escaped actual disease. Richard
Cadbury's heart ached to give them the chance of a week or
so in the peace and beauty of country surroundings, where
they would be cared for and have plenty of simple food and
good air and sleep.
(Richard Cadbury of Birmingham)

The Children's Hospital was in the centre of Birmingham, but there was nowhere nearby where the children could recover in the fresh air. The idea of a convalescent home on the outskirts of Birmingham started to form in Richard's mind. He didn't want it to feel like an institution, but to feel like a home-from-home filled with people who cared for the children. The family home at Moseley Hall covered 22 acres, and the lease was coming up for renewal but in case a buyer wasn't found for the entire estate, there were already plans in place to carve the land up for business purposes. Eventually, having discussed it with Emma and having found no other suitable location, Richard decided that this was the ideal place and he gave the home over for this purpose.

The cost of both the house and the land was large, and the building also needed alterations and a central heating system. But Richard was prepared to pay whatever he could in order to achieve this dream, and the management was handed over to the Children's Hospital who already had a small convalescent home. This one, at Arrowfield Top, was given up and the organisation was transferred to Moseley Hall. A Mr and Mrs Tomey, the matron and her husband, were to take charge. John Henry Lloyd, a friend of Richard's, was honorary secretary at the Children's Hospital. On 10 November 1890, he wrote a formal letter to Richard:

We have agreed to cordially accept your offer. I need hardly
say how deeply we feel your generosity, and how desirous
we are to unite with you in making the very best use of the
gift for the suffering poor children. I am afraid we shall
come in upon you like a flood, but almost all the members
of the committee are sure to want to see Moseley Hall; also
some ladies. Would 11a.m. on Friday be convenient to you
and Mrs. Cadbury? We do not wish to intrude too large a

number of the two committees. Do let me know the maximum
number you can do with processing around the house.

Richard Cadbury replied the very same day, by return:

I wish first of all to express how deeply I am indebted to you
for the kind personal interest you have taken in helping me
to carry through the desire I have so long had, to make this
place a home for the sick and suffering little children of this
town and neighbourhood. It seems difficult to realise that it
is now so near accomplishment. Friday morning will suit us
very well for those interested to see over the Hall, and all
that Mrs. Cadbury asks is that you would kindly send word
about the number you expect to come.

A number of other letters exchanged hands over the ensuing weeks,
mostly from Richard ensuring the finer details in order to make the
house a happy, comfortable home for the children.

The family moved into their new home shortly before Christmas 1891.
There was a formal opening of Moseley Hall for the convalescence of
children one Saturday afternoon. Richard handed the property over to
the Mayor of Birmingham and after a few words the home was declared
open. Initially it was intended as a place for sickly children who were
able to run about the place, with perhaps one or two who were bed-
bound. Gradually, though, it became a proper convalescent hospital
where children went after or in between medical operations. The staff
was expanded as necessary, with more medically qualified nursing staff
now employed.

On fine summer days the children would be carried out on
small wicker couches to lie under the shade of the trees, and
many a little face looked bright and happy that would have
pined and drooped in the close courts of the city. On indoor
days the large rooms of the old house made cheerful, airy
wards. An average of about sixty-two children often passed
through the Home in summer-time, and numbers would be
waiting to take their turn. Parents and friends have often
expressed their gratitude at the care given to their children.

One mother was so delighted with the change in her child
that at the end of the month she simply refused to take it out,
and did not rest till she had found friends willing to pay for
it for another month.

(*Richard Cadbury of Birmingham*)

The almshouses

During what turned out to be the last year of Richard's life, he was busy with his brother on another project. In 1897/8, thirty-three red-roofed bungalows were built on the corner of Maryvale Road and Linden Road, only 300 yards from the factory, around a quadrangle with a clock tower in the centre. These houses were built for elderly married couples or single people, with a preference for retired Cadbury employees. But as it turned out, these ex-workers were only a small percentage of those who ended up living in the almshouses. Each bungalow was completely self-contained with its own entrance, but with communal gardens. The grass quadrangle was dotted with flowerbeds and trees, and there was an old orchard at the back that used to belong to the old Bournbrook Hall.

There were some very specific rules about who could live in these houses. The almshouses were built to house two people, either a married couple or a mother and daughter, where one of the occupants had to be 60 years old or more. They had to have their own financial means, at least 5 shillings a week for a single person, or 7s 6d for a married couple, and their income was not to exceed £50 a year for a single person or £60 for a couple. Thirty-eight houses adjoined the almshouses and the rent from these dwellings were to go towards the upkeep of the almshouses.

Heating, lighting and medical attendance were provided free of charge to the residents of these bungalows, which had sleeping areas curtained-off from the living rooms, and a small kitchen. They were furnished with solid oak furniture and there were offices and a common room available for the tenants too. Shortly before what was to be Richard's last trip abroad, he had the honour of personally admitting the first six residents, although he did not live long enough to see them settled.

The houses are still standing today, numbered and signposted 1 – 33, and can be rented from the Bournville Village Trust. The railings around the complex were taken for the war effort during the Second World War and most were replaced again afterwards. There is, however, a small section that has been left to demonstrate how badly the stone work was damaged. Net curtains hang at the stone mullioned windows to keep out prying eyes. You can still see the factory in the background, but the quadrangle is gated with wrought iron gates to keep non-residents out. There is a little courtyard where staff cars can park outside the small offices. Both roads are very busy now, as there are shops and bus stops and many other houses crowded around. Yet despite this twenty-first century bustle, the houses still have a quiet, serene quality to them with no visible vandalism.

Chapter 9

Public service

Richard Cadbury wasn't only all about charity and religion, although both featured heavily in his life and the lives of his descendants. He also championed the cause of total abstinence, which didn't just come under the umbrella of his own religion. There were lots of temperance societies around in the 1800s. He was anti-war, which did come under his own religion, but he may have been a pacifist even had he not been a practising Quaker. All of this meant he was also involved with Liberalism and women's suffrage, his own actions being of the chivalrous kind rather than the chauvinistic.

Politician

Richard was a big fan of Gladstone, but he did disagree with the politician on some things. Birmingham had always leaned towards the Liberal, but during the 1880s, the Liberal Association was subject to two major blows. The first was when the treasurer died, the second when the secretary resigned. These two events put the future of the association at risk. One day Richard Cadbury bumped into one W. Finnemore in the street and said to him: 'I hear there is some chance of your coming to the Liberal Association. I am very interested to hear it. The work is so difficult and trying that I should hesitate to recommend you to do it; but, if you do, I shall be glad to help you, and I can speak for my brother also.' Finnemore did indeed take on the position of secretary, and he later wrote:

> *Needless to say, in face of the difficulties which Liberal work in Birmingham presented, that was a most comforting assurance, and he was as good as his word. We reorganised*

the association, and in the first year won the first political success that had been achieved, since the split in 1886, at a by-election for the ward of Ladywood. This delighted Mr. Cadbury very much. He was singularly broad-minded as a politician, and for political ends in which he believed was quite content to work with men from whom on other questions he strongly dissented. [...] The last communication I ever had from Mr. Cadbury was a letter saying how much he would like to help. He said he was then making preparations for a journey to the East, but asked me to see him immediately on his return. Alas! that time never came, and all good works in Birmingham and many elsewhere, suffered heavily by the great loss.
(*Richard Cadbury of Birmingham*)

Richard Cadbury held several public roles, including the following:

- In 1889, he was vice-chairman of the Liberal Association
- In 1890, he became vice-president of the Liberal Association
- He was president of the association from 1891 – 1897
- From 1895 – 1898, he was president of the Deritend Ward Liberal Club
- For many years he was president of the Birmingham branch of the National Vigilance Association
- In 1892, he was appointed as a Justice of the Peace for Birmingham
- And in 1895, he was asked to stand for parliament.

He agreed to stand for parliament only if the Liberal Association were unable to find another suitable candidate. They succeeded, and he gave the nominee his full support.

Temperance legislation was a subject close to Richard's heart, yet he could not support the Bishop of Chester's campaign to adopt the Gothenburg system as he felt it was a retrograde move and would not advance temperance reform. Already being utilised in Sweden and basically meaning 'the municipalisation of the liquor traffic, including the provision of model public-houses' (*Richard Cadbury of Birmingham*), Richard believed 'that it did not strike at the root of the evil of drunkenness; that it could not be proved to have reduced drinking in Sweden; that it did not provide any area free from the temptation of drink; that it did not protect the poor, while the rich were able to protect themselves, as in suburban building estates; that the licences, being annual, would receive a legalised vitality, and be more difficult to repress; and finally, that the effect and influence of passing the trade over to town and county councils would be to stimulate it, in order to reduce the rates, thus doing away entirely with any inducement for decreasing the sale'.

Richard did not simply reject the Gothenburg arrangement without giving it consideration. He had attended a meeting on the subject in his neighbour's house at Highbury, with Joseph Chamberlain and the Bishop of Chester. He had studied the results of prohibition in Maine, in the United States, and he had studied the successful regulation of drink in Toxteth Park in Liverpool. All of this became useful ammunition again when Richard championed Sir William Harcourt's Local Veto Bill in 1895, which, among other things, gave power to control both the character and the number of public houses to the local magistrates.

The Blue Ribbon Movement

Richard T. Booth was an American advocate of the temperance cause. He was a celebrity of the time and wherever he went interest in total abstinence rose sharply. In 1882, he toured the towns and cities of England on his gospel temperance crusade, which became known as the Blue Ribbon Movement, with those involved known as the Blue Ribbon Army. The movement drew a lot of attention to the evils of drinking and Booth was an accomplished speaker who knew how to rouse the crowds. Some say his followers fell under his spell.

Richard and George Cadbury watched this new movement with interest and decided that it would be good to get Richard Booth in Birmingham if they could. They wanted to draw together Christians of all denominations, not just Quakers, and they came up with a scheme, believing that Booth was the key:

> [...] it seemed [wise] *for a private individual to undertake the venture, rather than an official representative of any sect, or even of a temperance society.*

118

> *After due consideration, they therefore called in from the office at Bournville Edward Ward, a man in whose Christianity and temperance principles they had thorough confidence. They laid the scheme before him, saying they felt he was the right man to carry it out, and that they were only too willing to give him all the* [undecipherable] *that he would need. After much demur and hesitation on his part, and mutual prayer, Edward Ward decided to undertake the trust. The first step was to visit R.T. Booth's missions in other places. Armed with notes of introduction from Richard and George Cadbury, he visited first Leicester, and then Stockport. Having gained this practical experience, the next thing was to raise a private guarantee fund, so that he might not be blocked at every turn by the question from many who would sympathise with the effort. "Yes; but where is the money to come from?"*
>
> (*Richard Cadbury of Birmingham*)

Richard Cadbury went with Edward Ward to visit the wife of the mayor, who added her name to the list of subscriptions. Other prominent local families were visited, and in a very short time the necessary guarantee had been raised. Support from church ministers and other Christian representatives was also solicited and their names added to a circular that was distributed to all the free churches in the city. When support was sufficient, the Church of England was also enlisted.

The upshot was that a general committee was formed and an invitation sent out to Richard T. Booth to come to Birmingham. Curzon Hall was made ready, including new seating. With the cost of the refurbishment and also the printing costs, Richard Cadbury agreed to guarantee any monies that were outstanding at the end of the campaign. This turned out to be quite a large sum in the end, but he cheerfully cleared the balance when the time came. John Cadbury offered to host Mr and Mrs Booth, and thousands of small blue ribbons were prepared, to serve as a badge of total abstinence.

Richard T. Booth and his wife arrived in Birmingham on the afternoon of Tuesday, 16 May 1882 to a public welcome. Several carriages met them at the station and drove to Old Square, where a triumphal procession formed and paraded through the town. The accompanying carriage that

Richard Cadbury was pegged to ride in was over-full, however, but true to form, he simply insisted on walking behind. The procession was made up of various church representatives, which 'made its way down Corporation Street, New Street, High Street, and the Bull Ring', all of which are still there today.

The parade ended in the recently completed cattle market and a massive meeting was held indoors there, with many followers spilling outside into the street. Pledge cards started to appear in factories, shops and many private homes. There was a series of meetings held over the next three weeks, some of which were chaired by John Cadbury, while Richard Cadbury visited the homes of people who had signed the pledge.

> *More than sixty-six thousand persons adopted the blue ribbon badge as a sign of their total abstinence. Among this number were some who were teetotallers before the mission was held, but during the three weeks' campaign over fifty thousand new pledges were taken. A thorough and lasting work had been done, and a vital blow had been struck at the drinking customs of the time.*
>
> *(Richard Cadbury of Birmingham)*

At the end of the three weeks, some supporters worried that this might be the end of the cause, so Richard Cadbury suggested a permanent organisation, and the Gospel Temperance Mission was formed. Ultimately, he became chairman and treasurer of the new mission. The honorary secretary at this time later wrote:

> *Mr. Cadbury attended nearly every meeting of the committee, and took part in many of the meetings throughout the district. His true, earnest piety and deep faith in the power of prayer was such as created thorough earnestness in all the workers; thousands of pledges were taken and the signers visited. [...] It was pretty generally shown that the greatest hindrance to a man keeping his pledge was the very unsatisfactory condition of his home-life, and it was felt that means should be taken to reach the wives and mothers of the men.*

Mr. Cadbury suggested the holding of meetings for women in the afternoon, and that suitable ladies should be employed, who had tact and earnestness combined with a sympathetic nature, to have control of the classes formed and visit the members to encourage them to make their homes brighter and help their husbands and sons to keep the pledge and attend to the higher things of life.

[...] Lady superintendents were soon appointed, and as class followed class in quick succession, helpers were engaged to assist them, so that a large staff was ultimately appointed. The whole financial responsibility was undertaken by Mr. R. Cadbury.

(Richard Cadbury of Birmingham)

A Miss M.C. Brookes was the first lady to be appointed. She wrote:

In the year 1884, March 3rd, I was introduced to Mr. R. Cadbury by the late Mr. David Smith of the Bloomsbury Institution. He told me how anxious he was to commence some work in the east of Birmingham. The kind way that he received me made a lasting impression on my mind. Just after that I went to a meeting where Mr. Cadbury was present. I was a stranger and did not know any one. He left his own friends and came and talked to me, because he thought I was lonely. He taught me a lesson in that one act to be thoughtful for others.

(Richard Cadbury of Birmingham)

Soon afterwards, the women's meeting at Bloomsbury was started with around forty women, many of whom had previously been locked up for one reason or another. Richard Cadbury told Miss Brookes: 'Look for the worst, and do your best to help them.'

Good deeds

There is no question whether Richard Cadbury was a kind and generous gentleman. Throughout his time at the chocolate works in Birmingham, the welfare of the workers was one of the most important factors to him. He also felt responsible for them after they had left the company to strike out on their own.

One man who used to work at the factory had left to set up his own business, but the business had failed. The man was in great distress when Richard came upon him and asked what he could do. The man asked for bread for his children, as they were starving. 'You shall never want a loaf of bread as long as I live,' was Richard's response. He bought food for the man, paid his rent for seven years, and found him some casual work for 5 shillings a week.

Another time, one chap wrote to him to ask if he could borrow £3. Richard Cadbury replied that he never lent money to anyone ... and he enclosed a cheque for £3. And then there was the girl who was treated badly by the son of a wealthy personality in Birmingham. Richard contacted the boy's father and threatened a prosecution unless his son made provision for the girl's future. As a result, the girl was more than adequately provided for.

One day he was walking to the mission hall when he saw a woman struggling to take home a barrow filled with coal. He stepped in and wheeled the barrow home for her. On another occasion, an elderly lady was on her knees in prayer and it was obvious she couldn't get back up again. There were many onlookers, but only Richard approached her and lifted her to her feet.

In 1893, the Gospel Temperance Mission, which started out meeting in the old iron room, experienced a crisis after the secretary retired, and the religious element was gradually replaced with the provision of amusement and entertainment without first being agreed by any committee. Ultimately, it found itself in debt. Richard stepped in temporarily until a new secretary was appointed, and he personally paid off the debt before re-instigating prayer and religion once again. Once the mission was brought back to order and restored to its original purpose, one of the workers wrote:

> *For this, Mr. Richard Cadbury was entirely responsible, for he was constant in his prayers and attentive to every detail. He was never known to grow discouraged; in fact, it was he who would cheer the workers on to renewed efforts, and his 'Let us pray about it' was always effectual in stilling the troubled mind. Monthly prayer-meetings of the staff*

were held, and at these he was invariably present, presiding
over one of them the day before he sailed on his last voyage.
(Richard Cadbury of Birmingham)

A young 13-year-old girl who later went on to work at the Gospel
Temperance Mission went to see Richard Cadbury once, to ask for a
sovereign towards an upcoming Sunday school bazaar. She had walked all
the way to Bournville. Richard asked her who had sent her and she replied
that no one other than God had directed her to him. Richard asked her to
hold out her hands. In one hand he placed the requested sovereign and told
her that was for the bazaar. In the other hand he placed a shilling and a penny.
The shilling, he said, was for the girl, and the penny was for her fare back.

He would also send donations to churches that were struggling to
make ends meet, despite being quite cross in the way these debts were
sometimes incurred. But it appears he received many begging letters
from such organisations. When he was told that one church would have
found it impossible to continue its good work without getting into debt,
Richard wrote back:

> *I am sorry if I cast any reflection on the earnest and good*
> *work you are doing. I am one with you heart and soul, but*
> *these debts are such an awful drag on the Lord's work, and*
> *I contend quite unnecessary, for the Lord will make a way,*
> *where men are in earnest for His service. A correspondent,*
> *a splendid worker, this morning says, "Our church is doing*
> *a good work, but it will be able to do much more when*
> *relieved of this burden, which is as a millstone round our*
> *necks." Almost every letter of the kind (and I receive dozens*
> *in the week) are to this effect.*
>
> *(Richard Cadbury of Birmingham)*

Two men once called on Richard to ask for a donation to their Band of
Hope, which had got into financial difficulty. Richard apparently gave
them a good dressing down and they started to leave, feeling dejected at
the failure of their quest. Richard called one of them back and whispered:
'It's all right this time. Go on, and I will give you £100.' A hundred
pounds would have been quite a sum in the late 1800s, worth around
£12,743 in 2019, according to one CPI inflation calculator.

Two final addresses

During what was to be Richard Cadbury's last Christmas, aside from the usual family commitments in which he dressed up as Father Christmas, a new Friends' Hall and Institute on the Moseley Road was pretty much completed. A formal opening had been planned for May 1899 but, due to Richard's unexpected death in March, it never transpired. However, on 27 December 1898, a tea had been arranged at the new premises, which was attended by around 1,600 people, consisting of adult pupils and members of the other various Highgate concerns. Richard and Emma attended the event, along with Barrow Cadbury and his wife, Edith and her husband, William, Helen, Margaret, Beatrice and Alec. When Richard rose to speak, he was greeted with a deafening ovation, but eventually managed to present the following:

> *In wishing you all a happy new year I do so with heartfelt thankfulness for the blessings we have all received during this closing year of 1898, and with a sure hope that God will bless us in the future as we look to Him to guide us in the new and increased work and responsibilities that lie before us. This is not a formal opening to the public, but a Christmas welcome to all who have for a longer or shorter period worked with us through the past twenty years.*
>
> *It is in no sectarian spirit that we have welcomed the help of those who are willing to join with us in bringing in the wanderer and the outcast, in reforming the drunkard, and in holding forth the lamp of hope, faith, and charity to all who have not accepted God's means of salvation. Nor is it our desire to compete with other Christian churches and public bodies in building this house and institute for the people; but we believe that the homes of our artisans will be brighter and better for the influences brought to bear upon their moral and religious life in this place. Recreations and amusements are necessarily part of our social life, and one of the great problems of the day is to solve the question as to the best means of keeping them free from contamination of the moral character.*

Our work is to train the young into habits of industry, and to inculcate in them pure and holy thoughts, to stimulate social and intellectual intercourse among those growing into manhood and womanhood, so that their ambition shall be to encourage mutual respect for one another and to place love on its highest throne, by gentleness, by good report, by manly courage, by cultivating the mind, by earnest work, and by sanctified dedication to God's service.

We claim no superiority in these matters over others who are working on the same lines, but wish to emulate all in zeal and consecration. One great principle governs the children of God; that they are one in Christ. Some say and think that unity is impossible; well, if they think so they do not believe in Him Who said "that they all may be one as Thou Father art in Me, and I in Thee, that they also may be one in Us." It is on this principle alone that the men of the world will be won for Christ, and until the churches recognise this unity of believers there will be no great ingathering of the people. The reason is not far to seek; it is because the churches will be brought into sympathy with one another, for although they may differ from one another in outward forms, they will acknowledge Christ as the great Shepherd of His sheep, who says, "And there shall be one fold and one Shepherd."

Ours is a humble attempt to build upon the one foundation, without reference to creed or hierarchical pretensions. The Bible texts on these walls proclaim allegiance to the doctrine of the priesthood of believers and over the divinity of Christ.

We look forward to the new year for increased opportunities and zeal for His kingdom, and devoutly ask for His guidance and blessing upon all that is undertaken in His name.

(Richard Cadbury of Birmingham)

In these words, Richard Cadbury summed up his own life. Nobody could have put it any better. What he didn't expect was a presentation made back to him by those in attendance. A table, a reading desk, a large armchair, and eight other chairs intended for the platform were all made from oak and each inscribed with the letters 'R.C.' and the bundle of sticks Richard himself had chosen as the institute's emblem. He started to thank them for their presentation, but had to ask Emma to complete the acceptance speech for him as his own voice shook and broke with emotion.

A second trip had been planned to visit the Holy Land (see Chapter 10), but Richard worked right up until the very last day before the family left. He liked to tidy up any loose ends before he went away for any period of time, and one of the things that had been agreed was the plan to change Cadbury Brothers into a limited company should anything happen to either he or his brother George. The adult classes had been meeting in the new institute for the first few Sundays of the year, and on 29 January 1899, before leaving for the East, he gave an address to the entire school. The story was reported on, in a fashion, in the *Birmingham Weekly Mercury* under the headline 'The Silence of God':

He was interesting from the first, speaking with clearness, though his voice showed symptoms of wear; without mannerisms or deadly commonplaceness; with a cultured style and evidences of imagination and instinctive love of the sublime and beautiful in nature. He spoke of the still small voice; of the silence of God. We should know more of God's silence in proportion as we know more of the working of the Holy Spirit of God. That Spirit must have been felt by us in prayer, or we should have no faith in its efficacy. As we sang of the stars and the firmament our thoughts went back to the dawn of creation, when the Spirit of God brooded over the face of the waters – silently. Sin came into the world and the silence of God was broken. In the temple of Solomon we saw a wonderful symbol of the silence of God, Every piece of wood was hewed into shape before it came to the builders. No sound of an axe or hammer was heard there. All was done in silence. On the other hand, we knew that when the temple was destroyed it was done with axes and hammers. The world was full of noise and sin. For his part, he humbly desired that we might return to the quiet and peace associated with a purer form of earthly life. Passing along the history of time, there was the Flood.

Again the silent eye of God looked on. We need to realise the power of sin, and the power of the Evil One, who goes about seeking whom he may destroy. We all knew this; the difficulty was to apply it to ourselves. This could be done by the Spirit of God in our hearts. We must not rely upon each other, but on ourselves. Thus might we find grace and help in every time of need. Elijah for the moment lost faith. The voice of conscience came to him, the voice of God, "Where art thou, Elijah?" In like manner the voice of God had found out Adam. We wanted the voice of God in our hearts and consciences. When the still small voice was heard, the prophet wrapped his face in his mantle.

Did we realise the solemnity of the presence of God? Were we there to worship? It is a solemn thing to stand in that silent presence. We should do well to have more silence in our worship, to let the Lord come in. We had enough of the voices of men in the world, and in our daily avocations. The wisdom of men was nothing when compared with the wisdom of the Lord.

Thus did Mr. Richard Cadbury hold forth, his manner quiet, and even modest; his tone and general style that of a level-headed citizen whose religious faith was real, wholehearted, and immovable. The people sat very still, giving to every word the most respectful attention.

Richard took a mission meeting that same evening at the Bournville and Stirchley Institute and the following night he chaired a mass meeting for men in Central Hall in the town centre. On the morning of 1 February, he attended a meeting with the Gospel Temperance Mission, and on the evening he had to leave a family dinner early to attend another meeting. When he returned home later that night, he apparently threw his hat in the air and said to Emma: 'And now, hurrah for a long holiday!'

Chapter 10

A traveller to the end

Richard was addicted to travel. His youngest daughter Beatrice would remember him as giddy as a child in a sweet shop whenever the family was due to go away again. Wherever they went, they would still find a church to attend on a Sunday, with a Friends' meeting being the first choice where applicable. Even when the children went abroad for school or to carry out mission work, Richard would use it as another opportunity to travel, often visiting the family on the way to or from somewhere else. And he would literally travel anywhere. Nowhere was out of bounds.

Richard and Emma alike needed only the slightest excuse. When Barrow was approaching his eleventh birthday, his grandfather John Cadbury made known his wish to have the boy spend some time in Stuttgart, Germany, with an acquaintance of his, Emily Kölle, her son and two other boys. He considered this a great opportunity for Barrow to learn the German language and to experience school in Stuttgart. He wrote to the boy's parents while they were on one of their holidays in Devonshire researching the family history. It was on Barrow's actual birthday that the boy went off on his journey abroad with Frau Kölle and her son. The following summer, Richard and Emma, accompanied by Richard's sister Maria, travelled to Germany to visit him, and then went on to Switzerland. In 1881, Barrow and Jessie were taken by their parents to Switzerland. The following year, Richard Jr (or Bonny) went to stay with Frau Kölle in Stuttgart, and Richard and Emma visited him there, taking in a trip to the Black Forest at the same time.

Richard moved his family into Moseley Hall in Moseley in 1883. At about the same time, the Egypt and Palestine Exploration Societies were revealing what they had discovered in the ancient world, and Richard followed the revelations with increasing eagerness. As had become his tradition, he created a scrapbook and filled it with photographs of the relics and extracts from pages on Egyptian history. He also collected old books and manuscripts on the same topic.

He was without doubt a very hard worker. When he wasn't at the factory, he was at one of his adult classes or missions. When he wasn't doing social work, he was in church. So when he went on holiday he took time off and threw himself, and his family, into travelling. The only thing he didn't leave behind was God, although nor did he forget his other responsibilities back home. When the family were at the Lizard in Cornwall, he wrote to the secretary of the Gospel Temperance Mission:

> *August 8th, 1892.*
> *I have had you often in my thoughts, and praised God that the work goes on with satisfactory results. We are having a very happy, restful time here, for which I am truly thankful. The weather has been hot and fine up to this afternoon, and now I hear the fog-horn booming from the large lighthouse opposite our lodgings, to warn ships off a treacherous coast. I would that men would hear the gospel message and take heed to it as well as these vessels do.*

When they were in Towyn the following year, he wrote to the adult school in Highgate:

> *MY DEAR FELLOW TEACHERS AND SCHOLARS, – These are only a few lines to tell you how often I have thought of you during my absence, and how I am looking forward to meeting you next Sunday. This is a beautiful place with a long sandy beach and view over the sea, looking out to the west, where we see the sun sinking down to his rest every night among the tinted clouds and sky. Behind us are the mountains, above which Cader-Idris rises high into the clouds, more often than not having his white night-cap on. Nearly every day we have had two services on the sands for children. Mr. Josiah Spiers has come from London especially for the purpose. He was the first promoter of these children's services, and it is a pretty sight to see the children flocking round him from digging on the sand to hear something about the love of Jesus. Some of them (almost all*

children of well-to-do parents), have never been spoken to about the need of forgiveness and salvation, and I am so thankful to say that many *have confessed Christ; some who came to laugh can now thank God that they have found Jesus to be* their *Saviour. I shall be with you in thought and prayer to-morrow morning, and trust that God will send you a rich blessing on your labours.*

Yours affectionately.
RICHARD CADBURY.

A popular run out for all of the family was a drive to the Lickey Hills in Bromsgrove. This country park dates back to Neolithic times, although it wasn't a designated country park until much more recently, and was once used by the Romans to transport salt. It was a royal hunting ground until the early 1680s, when the crown sold the Norman manor to the Earl of Plymouth. The earl and his family managed the land for the locals for the next 250 years. Along came the Victorians, who developed the area at around the time when the Cadburys came to visit. In 1888, the Birmingham Society for the Preservation of Open Spaces bought some of the land and handed it over to the City of Birmingham to manage.

Another regular trip was a spring holiday in Malvern, where there is also a range of hills, this time dating back to the Iron Age at British Camp, an Iron Age fort. The Normans built a monastery here that lasted until the Dissolution in the 1530s, but the area survived the English Civil War pretty much unscathed. The Victorians exploited the pure spring water when 'taking the waters' became fashionable. Charles Dickens and Charles Darwin both visited the town, and Edward Elgar, the great composer, lived here from 1898 until 1903, which would have been just after the family's visits here.

Malvern was still a favourite holiday destination, and each year the family would also decamp to the family of Emma Cadbury in Mansfield for a fortnight. They visited the Isle of Wight too, as well as Devonshire – the ancestral home. One year at a farmhouse near Ilfracombe in North Devon, the family had boiled eggs for breakfast. When they were finished, Richard turned the empty egg shells upside down and drew Humpty Dumptys on them. When they visited the same farmhouse a few weeks later, these Humpty Dumptys sat in a row inside a glass cupboard staring out at them.

In 1887, Richard and his brother George bought Wynds Point, the home of the soprano Jenny Lind until her death. The house stood close to British Camp at the foot of the Herefordshire Beacon in the Malvern range. From here the family could see the Welsh mountains to the west and across Bredon Hill towards Tewkesbury in the other direction. It was also possible to see the spires of three cathedrals and an abbey: Gloucester Cathedral; Worcester Cathedral; Hereford Cathedral; and Tewkesbury Abbey.

> *It soon became a tradition that each spring the Cadbury family would decamp to the house for three or four weeks at a stretch. Richard was in his element striding up the hilltops of Malvern, where he would stand with his coat open wide and arms spread out, declaring, "There is no air anywhere like Malvern air!"*
>
> *(Beatrice: The Cadbury Heiress Who Gave Away Her Fortune)*

During one visit to Wynds Point, on 4 February 1898, Richard wrote to one of his older daughters:

> *The hills are white with snow. It was snowing all morning, but was fine for Daisy, Beatrice, and Alec, who came this afternoon. We went for a walk this evening by moonlight. It was gloriously fresh, and on our return we found the roads hard with frost. The gorse is yellow with flower, and one rose-tree is green with young leaves. I think the rest is doing dear mother good. I am thankful to say that I am strong and full of vigour; these fresh winds blow strength into me.*
>
> *(Richard Cadbury of Birmingham)*

The air at the Malvern Hills has always been known to be good, with sickly children being sent there to the open air hospital during the early twentieth century. It is particularly "clean" the higher the visitor climbs and is known to assist breathing conditions, such as mild asthma. There are natural springs dotted all over too, pouring and spurting out clean and pure spring water.

When they weren't marching about the Malvern hills, the family would cycle to nearby Tewkesbury for breakfast in a hotel close to the abbey. They entertained celebrities at Wynds Point, such as George Bernard Shaw and Ramsay MacDonald, and they would discuss the various affairs of the day, such as the Trafalgar riots in 1886, which Beatrice possibly listened to but probably did not understand at the time (*Beatrice: The Cadbury Heiress Who Gave Away Her Fortune*).

Some holidays were spent in Wales, climbing Cader Idris, and another was over in Ireland, on the west coast. Of their holiday in Kirklee in Ireland Beatrice remembered, in her biography of her mother:

> *There was a row of bathing-machines where you undressed for bathing. These were pulled into the sea, so that we could step down from them into the water tidily arrayed in our bathing-dresses and hidden from prying eyes. After our bathe the bathing-machine was pulled up again by a horse into the sands and we could later emerge, full dressed, ready to walk, play, build castles in the sand or generally amuse ourselves.*
>
> (*Emma Richard Cadbury: 1846 – 1907*)

Another family holiday was spent in Scotland. Beatrice again remembered:

> *A holiday some years later was spent near Gairloch on the north-west coast of Scotland, opposite the Isle of Skye. The cottage where we were to stay was isolated and lay in a small bay. We had driven nearly thirty miles from the nearest railway station and were put down on the road with our big baskets of linen and table silver, until we could get a cart to take our baggage across the strip of sand to the cottage on the other side.*
>
> (*Emma Richard Cadbury: 1846 – 1907*)

Then there was Cornwall when the family stayed at the Lizard and would walk every day between cornfields to Kynance Cove, where they would stay all day and play, before walking back. On all of their holidays they would find a church or a chapel for Sunday worship, and Richard was often asked to speak. Even in Switzerland.

When Richard's sister Maria moved to Boulogne-sur-Mer in France, the family had another holiday destination. Helen remembered in her biography of her father: *North Wales, the coast of Cornwall, Scotland, the Yorkshire moors, and of course Malvern, were favourite haunts of the family. There were flying visits, too, to the home of Richard Cadbury's sister, Maria, in Boulogne-sur-Mer.*

The boat trip from Dover to Calais followed by a rail journey to the small fishing town was another adventure: *We sometimes went to a small restaurant by the railway line, to watch the express train thunder past from Calais to Paris. That train carried the whole family a year or two later to Paris and Switzerland.* (*Emma Richard Cadbury: 1846 – 1907*)

Switzerland, of course, was a familiar stomping ground for Richard as he had spent his youth travelling there. When he returned with his family, they were able to spend several weeks revisiting his favourite places, going on guided walks and climbing mountains. Richard even enjoyed a surprise meeting with one of his old guides. The snow was so deep the guide had to remind the travellers to walk lightly and use their alpine sticks. In a small hut on top of the pass there was hot chocolate available, which was very much appreciated in the extreme cold. When Richard visited Switzerland in 1894 with his wife and all five of his daughters, he became known as the 'gentleman travelling with six ladies'. On this trip he took great pleasure in taking them to his old haunts, showing them the sights, revisiting old memories and making new ones.

In August 1895, Richard was in Scotland and he once again wrote to the secretary of the Gospel Temperance Mission:

August 8th, 1895.
It is interesting to know that all is going on well. Our plodding work among the masses will have its reward, with faith and patience to persevere. We are having a very happy time here, beyond the arena and strife of tongues and newspaper articles. Our landlord is a fine specimen of a Highlander, in his kilt and native dress – a sound Liberal and an abstainer. We are close to the sea in a little bay, and all around us the mountains covered with heather or timber; I think it is the most beautiful place I was ever in.

August 10th.

There is no public-house in Gairloch, and everything breathes peace. No one seems to suspect any one else of dishonesty or roguery. I found once we had gone to bed with the front door wide open all night, and our landlord said there was no fear at all from any one in the neighbourhood. I sometimes wonder when all men will thus have faith in one another! Our work is in the right direction, although it seems but a trifle amongst the selfishness, distrust, and wickedness around us. May we have that perfect faith in one another, in which alone we shall find strength, in God's name to bring light and happiness to those who live in darkness. Mazzini says, "We are here on earth not to contemplate, but to transform created things, to found, as far as in us lies, the image of the Kingdom of God on earth." And another writer, "Each word we speak has infinite effects, each soul we pass must go to heaven or hell, and this our one chance through eternity."

It is wonderful how bracing the air is here, and there is so much to interest in the plants, and flowers; sea and land birds also in infinite variety. The mountains raise from 1,000 to over 3,000 feet in height, so that there is plenty of climbing to do, and there are lots of boats on the lochs.

In 1896, Richard, Emma and three of the children visited Italy. They went to Rome, Milan, Naples, Florence and Pompeii. In those days, they were still doing much of the excavation work at Pompeii that seems to be taken for granted today. It must have been a very exciting time. Richard Jr had recently arrived in South Africa, where he was to learn more about fruit farming. His father wrote to him from Italy:

March 24th, 1896.

We have been hard at work among the beauty of the Italian lakes. We saw, in Milan, the original picture of Leonardo da Vinci, 'The Last Supper'; and then on to Rome with its treasures of the past [...] Here we are now among the beautiful work of the men that made Florence: Michelangelo, Dante, Savonarola, Galileo and Della Robbia and other great men.

(*Emma Richard Cadbury: 1846 – 1907*)

In early 1897, the bulk of the family made their first trip to Egypt and Palestine. Richard had read much about these destinations and longed to visit. Indeed, Thomas Cook had recently started to arrange excursions there. The Cadburys travelled by train and by boat and by train again, and Richard suffered badly with travel sickness. They stayed at the Shepheard's Hotel in Cairo, from where they visited the pyramids. The tourists were dragged up the side of and through the narrow tunnels of the pyramids by their over-eager guides, and they enjoyed camel rides. At that time the Sphinx had not been fully uncovered and only its head and eyes peered over the surface of the sand across the desert, whilst the tomb of Tutankhamen was not even a pipe-dream. Trips up the River Nile were made by the *Ramesses II*, a small steamer with the capacity to carry up to fifty passengers.

When they were done with Cairo, the family moved on to Jaffa in Palestine, again by boat. Two days after leaving Cairo, they dropped anchor just outside the harbour and waited for smaller boats to arrive and row them to shore. In Jaffa they enjoyed the delicious fruit grown in the orange groves before continuing on their journey to Jerusalem. Here they stayed at the Grand Hotel and they went by horseback to the Dead Sea via Jericho, where they floated in the surreal waters. While they were on this trip, Richard and Emma kept a travel journal. They arrived in Jaffa on 3 March, and Emma wrote:

> *Our first view of Jaffa, as we stood on the deck of the ship, was beautiful. It stands on low hills, dipping into the Mediterranean, and behind the town we could see the plain of Sharon, and the hills of Samaria and Judea.*

And a day later:

> *Quite suddenly our carriages drove through the Jaffa gate, and we were in Jerusalem! We were all quiet; our hearts were too full to talk, for it seemed so strange and wonderful to be in the city of which from babyhood we had heard and read and sung.*

From Jerusalem, the family went on a massive camping trip, packing three sleeping tents, a kitchen tent and a dining tent onto the backs of mules. During a severe hailstorm, their horses refused to go on, and they camped in a quagmire at Bethel while the thunderstorms continued through the night, eventually forcing them to seek refuge in a nearby monastery. After the storm the adventure continued on foot and the family camped on the banks of Lake Galilee near to the hot springs there. Once again, they were deluged with storms. And once again, they sought refuge in a monastery.

Caroline Cadbury, a cousin of Richard's, was working at the Friends' Mission in Brummana, not far from Beirut, so the family made the journey by train from Damascus, and open carriages took them from the station to the mission. From here the family were able to gaze out across the Mediterranean Sea towards the mountains of Cyprus and watch the fishing boats bobbing on the water as the fishermen dived for sea sponges. On the return voyage home, Richard wrote in the journal:

> *Our last few days were spent at Brumana among our dear friends on the Lebanon. It is a lovely spot, and is free from the control of the Sultan, although Beyrout [sic] and Damascus are under his sway. Friends are doing a novel work, both there and in the neighbouring villages. Their schools for boys and girls and their hospital are full. The latter is far too small for the requirements of the people, as it is the only one for the half-million who live on Lebanon. It was so interesting to see and hear native Christians take part in the meetings, just as we should do in England. Both the meetings I attended were full, and great attention was paid to what was said. I ventured to speak at both through an interpreter. We are returning in health with thankful hearts, having had a delightful tour, and one that I hope will be useful to us all.*

The last holiday in England of Richard's life was spent in Cornwall, with the three youngest girls, Helen, Margaret and Beatrice, and also Edith, with her husband and own baby boy. There is more about the family's various holidays and travels in Appendix II, from the personal point of view of Beatrice, the baby of the family – in her own words.

A life cut short

The family had such a wonderful time in Egypt and Palestine in 1897 that they decided to return two years later. The first trip had achieved

Richard's main objective of bringing the Bible to life, and he was itching to go back. Other interesting sites had been discovered or new access had been granted to the public since their previous trip and their itinerary was adapted to fit many of these in, including the second cataract of the River Nile, which is now submerged beneath Lake Nasser. This time, Richard and Emma's new son-in-law, Arnold Butler, joined the party and, on 2 February 1899, a large family gathering met at New Street Station in Birmingham to see them safely on their journey.

Once again, the travellers kept a journal of their trip. They visited the same places as before and travelled by steamer along the River Nile, eventually joining a second steamer at Assuan to the second cataract of the Nile, and on to Abousir. After a visit to Wady Halfa, where they came upon a lion cub, tied up like a dog yet as 'playful as a kitten', Emma wrote in the journal:

> *We are all in the best of health, and enjoying everything thoroughly. I wish you could all see father; he is most enthusiastic, taking rubbings and drawings wherever he can. Every one comes to him for information, and he is looked on as "the Egyptologist" on the boats. He joins in everything that is going on, and chats with all.*

While they were in Assiut, the party visited an American mission they had seen on their previous journey. By now, two years later, the 'hospital' comprised two huts joined together and was reached via some narrow and quite dirty streets. Inside the courtyard, Richard commented on a horrible smell but as usual, he rolled up his sleeves, figuratively speaking, and joined in with the work. The next day he complained of a sore throat, and soon after Helen was complaining of the same condition, followed by little Beatrice. By the time they made their return journey to Cairo, it was clear that several of the party had been infected by what was originally thought to be a condition known locally as Nile Throat. Richard and Helen were both quite unwell, but the doctor assured them that they were all well enough to travel. A week later, when Richard, Helen and Beatrice were declared fit to travel once again, they left the Shepheard's Hotel in Cairo and continued on to Jerusalem.

Richard became very ill at the hotel in Jaffa Gate where they had stayed on the earlier visit. It was only later that the family learnt he had actually contracted diphtheria. On the last evening, Richard and Emma read the Bible together, said a prayer, and Richard drifted off to sleep. In the early hours of the morning, he suffered a heart attack and never regained consciousness. The family were devastated and could hardly believe he was gone. Only a few days before he had written a letter to his adult class back home in Birmingham:

> *My dear friends, we are a long distance apart but feel sure that our thoughts and prayers bring us very near-together. We are about 450 miles from Cairo on this wonderful river which flows through a desert land.*
> *(Beatrice: The Cadbury Heiress Who Gave Away Her Fortune)*

Richard had made it very clear that he wanted to be buried in the relatively new cemetery in Selly Oak, Birmingham, and Emma wanted to carry out this wish. His body was taken to the hospital in Jerusalem then repatriated a month later. He was buried at Lodge Hill, as per his wish, on Saturday, 8 April 1899. Richard's funeral was attended by a great number of people from far and wide, so well thought of and loved was he.

Richard Cadbury died on 22 March 1899. He was 63. His loss was felt very keenly by those who knew him. A.G. Gardiner wrote:

> *He carried the sunshine with him wherever he went, and combined a simple and unaffected piety with a constant good humour and practical helpfulness that made him universally loved. His life had been a record of incessant service, and his benefactions were not less generous and widespread than those of his brother, though they followed an earlier model, and aimed at stimulating social reform and shaping opinion on such subjects as the land and old age pensions, than at alleviating the misery he saw around him. No good cause in Birmingham appealed to him in vain, and among his many considerable gifts to the public were the conversion of his old home, Moseley Hall, into a convalescent home for children; the erection and foundation of the beautiful almshouses at Bournville;*

and the building of the Moseley Road Institute for the Adult School movement. His interests were various, but they were all permeated by the one dominating passion of his life, the desire to win men to the faith which shone with such steady radiance in himself.

(Life of George Cadbury)

Together, Richard and his brother George had formed one of the closest, strongest comradeships in business for forty years, each complementing the other. While George was the daring one, Richard was more balanced, but both put the business and the welfare of their workforce, and those around them, to the fore.

Richard Cadbury was remembered as a courteous man. Tom Hackett again remembers:

One of the things for which Mr. Richard was admired was the willingness with which he came back to apologise for any hasty remark he may have made, and I always considered this to be one of the graces of his character, and one well worth of imitation.

(A History of Cadbury)

One of the many workers who had known and loved Richard Cadbury wrote a letter to the local paper:

Will you permit me, as one who has been employed for a long period of years by the firm of which Mr. Cadbury was the senior member, to bear my witness to his great worth and goodness. In business life he was an object-lesson to all his people. Punctual, alert, quick to understand the bearing of any subject brought before his notice, giving attention to small details, as well as deciding large issues in connection with a gigantic concern – in these and many other respects he was a model business man. His energy and buoyancy of spirit were contagious, and gave impetus to the despatch of business, which was felt though all departments. His cheery smile and pleasant word will long live in the memory of the firm's employees. When occasion called for reprimand

and censure, he did not fail to administer them; but if at any time it were shown to him that his judgment [sic] had been hasty and not well founded, no one could have been more ready to make amends. He was approachable by all, and the youngest boy or girl employed at Bournville felt this, and knew that "Mr. Richard" would listen to anything they desired to say.

When news of Richard's death reached Cornwall, a popular holiday destination for the family, the following appeared in a Penzance newspaper:

Many Cornishmen are to-day mourning the loss of one of the best and truest men this world has ever known.

His kindly presence, sunny disposition, and boyish lightheartedness endeared him to one and all, and he loved to roam over the downs, cliffs and shore, chatting with villagers, coastguards, and fishermen.

The death of such a man is a national loss, and his life a national lesson. Few men exercised a more far-reaching influence for good, and amongst the thousands who are mourning his loss, none will feel more genuine sorrow than those Cornish folk with whom he came into contact during his holiday visits to the Lizard district of the old county.

(Richard Cadbury of Birmingham)

From the female superintendent at the Gospel Temperance Mission came the following:

R emembered still! memories of thee
I nspired me with greater zeal to labour on for
C hrist; to extend His kingdom and glorify
H is name. Truly thy works follow thee.
A ll thy kindly words and wise counsels still
R emain. Thy presence ever brought gladness, always
D oing good for thy fellow man; to uplift and
C heer the sad – such was thine
A im while here on earth; these memories can never

D ie. Years may pass, change and decay must come;
B ut the influence of thy gentle,
U nselfish life, and noble deeds lives on.
R evered and loved by all who knew thee.
Y ea: thou art, indeed, remembered still!
                        (Richard Cadbury of Birmingham)

The following is taken from a page pasted into the family book, probably put there by William Cadbury, as it was William who took upon the responsibility for what is also known as *The Cadbury Pedigree* after his father's death. There is no information about the source of the cutting, but it was one of very many tributes to the late Richard Cadbury:

THE death of Mr. Richard Cadbury, which occurred at Jerusalem, is a great loss to religious and philanthropic life in the Midlands, and indeed in the whole country. Mr. Cadbury, who was his brother's partner in the great business at Bournville, was in his sixty-fourth year. His health was vigorous, his step light and buoyant, his heart brave and cheerful, and his friends might have looked with confidence to his attainment of three score years and ten, at least. But it was not to be, and they bow in resignation to the stroke which has deprived them of a whole-hearted, open-handed wise man.

Mr. Cadbury devoted himself with all his heart and soul and mind to the service of his generation. He loved quiet and retiring ways, but this did not prevent his name from becoming a household word in Birmingham. He had a burning love for little children. Thirty years ago he established a crèche – perhaps his first independent act of philanthropy. It would take almost a page merely to enumerate the institutions which he helped or created. The Friends' Hall and Institute is the outcome of Mr. Cadbury's enthusiasm as an educationist. He started the Severn Street Adult First Day Schools some twenty years ago with less than a dozen pupils. The work flourished exceedingly, and when the Institute was opened the roll contained the names of over 1,000 men, nearly 500 women, and about

1,350 junior scholars. Mr. Cadbury and his pupils made a great happy family. Three years ago, he and Mrs. Cadbury celebrated their silver wedding, and received many handsome gifts from the pupils. It was noticed at the time that Mr. Cadbury was far from well. He took a holiday in Palestine and came back much better. When his health again became impaired, he sought the same solace, but alas, he did not return alive. He was to have been formally welcomed home on the 1st of May. Mr. Cadbury's attitude to all his scholars was brotherly. The men's school met at seven o'clock on Sunday morning, and Mr. Cadbury was never late. After the meeting he breakfasted with his officers and members. He had to rise very early and walk from his beautiful home to the squalid neighbourhood of Highbury [sic – this should be Highgate, as Highbury was the far from squalid adjoining property to the house at Uffculme]. *The grounds of Uffculme, where Mr. Cadbury lived, border upon those of Highbury, the home of Joseph Chamberlain.*

Mr. Cadbury was on the best of terms with his work-people. He loved Birmingham, and endowed her richly. He spent £33,000 on the Moseley Hall Convalescent Home for children, and this is only one of many benefactions. He is a Liberal in politics and loves peace [sic – the reporter seems to have slipped into the present tense here]. *He took a deep interest in the formation of the National Free Church Council and was a generous contributor to its funds. His attachment to the Society of Friends was rooted and reasoned. He wrote an able summary of their tenets in a neat little book, entitled "What is my faith?" which has had a large circulation.*

Mr. Cadbury's love for children showed itself markedly three years ago when he gave a Bible to each scholar under the Birmingham School Board who was above the third standard. This meant a distribution of nearly 20,000 Bibles and an expenditure of £1,300. He received hundreds of spontaneous letters of thanks from the children. Some of them were quaint. One boy hoped that Mr. Cadbury would be "a good and prosperous man." One grave little man – or woman – offered congratulations to Mr. Cadbury because he had "found a better way of spending your money than on horse-racing." "One of your Chocolate Eaters" was the signature of another letter. To possess the love of little children is a handsome testimonial – no man ever enjoyed more of it than Mr. Cadbury.

He will long remain a gracious memory. The fruit of his work and worth will not diminish with the passing of the years. But Birmingham and the Free Churches throughout the country will sorely miss him for many a day. A man like Richard Cadbury is ill-spared, whether his life be short or long[.]

Emma battled on alone as best she could, with the help of both William and Helen. William still lived at home and Helen returned to help her mother, but Emma struggled to come to terms with what had happened, believing that her husband had been taken in his prime. She still enjoyed travelling and in 1907 she headed to the Far East again to visit the Bradleys, who were carrying out medical mission work in China. It was while she was at sea during a particularly rough storm that an otherwise healthy Emma Cadbury slipped and was thrown backwards on a staircase. She was knocked unconscious and, after a short period of apparent delirium, she too passed away. It is ironic to know that Emma was caring for a young girl who was dangerously ill when she had her accident. The boat had crossed the date-line in the ocean twice and the date was the second 21 May of 1907. Once again, the Cadburys had to repatriate a member of the family.

Emma was buried beside her husband in Lodge Hill Cemetery, Selly Oak. Reunited after eight lonely years.

Author's Note

When I was researching *A History of Cadbury*, I was frustrated to find that there wasn't really a lot about the older of the two Cadbury brothers in print, yet he seemed to be such a kind and interesting man. And so I took it upon myself to dig deeper to see what else I could learn about him. With the help of his great-granddaughter Mary Penny, granddaughter of William A. Cadbury, I soon realised I had done the right thing.

Richard Cadbury squeezed a lot into his relatively short life. He did what he could to alleviate conditions for the poor. He strove to ensure his workers had a good and healthy standard of living and that they were provided for in their retirement. He wasn't just a businessman who owned a half share in a chocolate factory. He was a father figure who cared for his workers. He was a philanthropist who wanted to share his wealth. He was a Quaker. He was a public figure, a potential politician. He was a good and kind person. And above all, he was a family man with seven children.

Richard Barrow Cadbury *was* a good man, and I hope I have done him and his memory justice.

The topic of the Gospel Temperance Mission would fill an entire volume. Quakerism would fill another. The Adult School Movement yet another. And so on. Yet, as Richard himself did so, we can only touch on such subjects without going into a lot of detail. There is also the story of his daughter Helen's struggle with her faith that could be covered in so much more detail, but that, perhaps, is Helen's story and not her father's. Again, it has been touched on briefly here.

Appendices

Appendix I

Richard Cadbury's sister, Maria, remembered her childhood fondly. Her recollections and some from her brother, Richard, are reproduced in both Helen Alexander's *Richard Cadbury of Birmingham* and A.G. Gardiner's *Life of George Cadbury*. (Reproduced by kind permission of the family.)

[...] Many were the games we had on the square lawn. Our father measured round it 21 times for a mile, where we used to run, one after another with our hoops before breakfast, seldom letting them drop before reaching the mile, and sometimes a mile-and-a-half, which Richard generally did. How rosy we were, seated round the breakfast-table ready for the basin of milk provided for each child, with delicious cream on the top and toast to dip into it. Our father went for a walk each morning, starting about seven o'clock, taking his dogs with him, and we were often his companions. The roads round Edgbaston were very country-like then, with rambles across fields, and pools of water where the dogs enjoyed a swim. One pretty walk was across the fields to Ladywood House, now in Vincent Street, in the midst of the town. We returned home to breakfast punctually at eight o'clock. The family Bible reading followed, and by nine o'clock our father was ready to start for business. I can picture his rosy countenance, full of health and vigour – his Quaker dress very neat with its clean white cravat. Our dear mother was always ready to see him off with a parting kiss. At nine o'clock the school bell rang, before which we generally had a run in the garden, and the boys a game on the gymnastic poles of various kinds, one as high as a

ship's mast, up which they all learned to climb. Richard was particularly clever in performing various antics on the bars. Our natural longing for music was so far encouraged that we were allowed to buy Jew's harps with our pocket money. These we thoroughly enjoyed, having learned several Scotch airs from hearing our mother singing them. We loved to listen to the sweet lullabies, with which she hushed the babies to sleep. Our father had two musical boxes in a special drawer in the bookcase. It was a great treat to us when he wound those up for our pleasure. Our grandfather and grandmother and Aunts Maria and Ann lived not far from our house, lower down in the Calthorpe Road. Many are the happy memories of running in to see them. The door key was hung outside. I can picture grandfather, standing before the dining-room mirror, very upright, seeing that his cravat was neat and coat collar well pulled up, and gloves ready, before starting to town; a piece of honeysuckle or southernwood or some sweet-scented spray put into the button-hole of his coat. We only knew our dear grandmother as aged and infirm, so cannot speak of the time when, as we have been told, her life was full of activities at home and among the sick and poor. We used to run into the fresh kitchen in the summer time to find our aunts in their clean morning dresses of print, and tall, white caps, busy getting up their muslins.

Our mother had a busy home life with her five boys and one girl. She was a lovingly watchful and affectionate wife and mother, seldom visiting from home. Although of a retiring disposition, she had a sound judgement, and was not easily moved, when she saw a thing to be right. She was gentle but firm with her children, and they were all devotedly fond of her. She had a great dread of exaggeration. My father has told me that when he was going to a public meeting to speak she used to warn him, when telling an anecdote, not to embellish, but to keep to the true facts. She and our father taught us to speak respectfully and pleasantly to all in their employment, for they liked those who lived with them to feel their house a home. The hymn "Speak Gently" was one my mother wished us to learn by heart when children, and I believe it had a wonderful influence upon us. We can never forget the tiny room where our mother used to retire, and where she gained much heavenly wisdom and strength with the Bible before her. I never remember our parents threatening us with a punishment they did not intend to carry out, or punishing hastily, or in a temper.

First day [Sunday] *was a happy one. We were taken to meeting as soon as we were old enough. When ready to start we would come down to father, and, standing by his side, he made Gray's "Elegy" with its illustrations very attractive, drawing interesting lessons. In one picture a bigger boy had broken the wheel of his little brother's cart to tease him. Another sturdy little fellow defends and sympathizes with the small child, Our father's lessons from that picture were never forgotten, and our eyes filled with tears when he talked to us about it. We always thought the kind, sturdy boy was like our brother Richard.*

In the old Meeting House in Bull Street an aisle went up the centre, the men sitting on the left-hand side and the women on the right. My five brothers sat in a row on the second form from the top, father facing them from his seat below the Minister's gallery, while I sat by my mother. We were brought up from childhood to go to Bull Street Meeting on a Fourth Day [Wednesday] *morning, so we had only afternoon school that day. Our father also closed his place of business in Bull Street for an hour or two, so that he and several young men Friends in his employ could attend Meeting* [...] *Our home was one of sunshine. Our parents doing all they could to make us happy, and the consistency of their own lives was a great help in forming the characters and tastes of their children. Home was the centre of attraction to us all, and simple home pleasures our greatest joy.*

[...] *Our favourite seaside place was the village of Blackpool. The quiet cottage on the shore where we stayed, on the south side, called Bonny's Cottage, had the greatest charm. We ran wild and built wonderful* [sand] *castles on the shore. I remember an unusually fine castle, which John and Richard built, and how active George was helping them. They made an erection of stones, and I was employed with the two younger boys, getting clay to fasten them together, mother also helping me to make a gay flag, which we fastened on to a long pole and placed on top of the fortress. The Blackpool seas were then, as now, very boisterous, and the boys were determined, if possible, to build a castle that could resist their strength, and they succeeded; theirs was the only one on the shore that stood after a heavy sea, but some mean-spirited boys went and cut down their flag-staff.*

Appendix II

Richard Cadbury was a great traveller. His youngest daughter, Beatrice, wrote a history of the life of her mother, Emma, in which she remembered many of the family's holidays. This biography was privately published. Extracts of her memories appear below. (Reproduced by kind permission of the family.)

HOLIDAYS AND TRAVELS
My father was like a boy let out from school at the approach of the holidays and my mother enjoyed them no less. The holidays were like an extension of their honeymoon and as the children came, their joy was enhanced by having them with them on these holiday occasions.

So it is that they will always remain among my most precious memories. Often in the summer the whole family would drive out to the Lickey Hills. How long and lovely was the drive along the Bristol Road between fields and hedges, till we reached the village of Rednal. We climbed the hills, played among the trees and sought for bilberries and ended up with tea at Rosemary Cottage, with its rose covered porch and low ceilinged room with its dark oak beams.

Almost always in the spring Malvern was the place for the family holiday. I can remember staying in Great Malvern and running up to St. Ann's Well before breakfast for a drink of the pure, cold water flowing into the little marble basin.

How both Father and Mother loved Malvern. As I think of those long ago days, I can see them, standing on top of one of the hills, side by side. Father would throw open his coat and spread his arms, while the wind blew his beard. –

'There's no air anywhere like Malvern air' he would exclaim. Later holidays were spent in West Malvern at Dorbar's farm. To reach it we had to go down a very steep hill and, beyond the farm, stretched the Ridge, rising ground tree-covered, where we walked and looked for primroses and violets, or where we lay reading or dozing under the trees.

In 1897 Father and Uncle George bought Wynd's Point, at the end of Worcestershire Beacon range and at the foot of the Herefordshire Beacon. This was also called the British Camp because of the grass-grown ramparts round the top, which the early Britons had built as a defence against the raids of the wild Welshmen from the mountains far west across the wide valley. How we all loved Wynd's Point. It had been the last home of Jenny Lind, the popular and much loved Swedish singer, who died there and is buried in the churchyard of Little Malvern Church below the deep wooded slope of the hills. From the garden-room, built above the old quarry, we could see the Welsh mountains to the West, and on the other side over the wide plain Bredon Hill behind Tewkesbury. On a clear day it was possible to make out the spires of three cathedrals; Gloucester, Hereford and Worcester, and also the tower of Tewkesbury Abbey. One summer we were reading Stevenson's Treasure Island and thenceforth the 'Lookout' above the quarry became for us, and always remained, 'The Jolly Jenny'. One of our much loved excursions was to get up early and ride to Tewkesbury on our bicycles for breakfast in a hotel near the abbey. I remember one occasion when it poured with rain all the way there and back! On our return Mother packed us off to bed to get warm and dry and to avoid colds.

Several holidays were spent in Wales, of which I remember the one at Colwyn Bay the best. We climbed Cader Idris from there and got caught in a mist coming down, so that we waited for some time, until the mist rose and we could see how to go farther.

One long summer holiday was spent at Kilkee on the west coast of Ireland. A row of boarding-houses stretched along the road, just above the sands where the great waves of the Atlantic came rolling in and broke along the beach. There was a row of bathing-machines where you undressed for bathing. These were pulled into the sea, so that we could step down from them into the water tidily arrayed in our bathing-dresses and hidden from prying eyes. After our bathe the bathing-machine was pulled up again by a horse into the sands and we could later emerge, fully dressed, ready to walk, play, build castles in the sand or generally amuse ourselves.

A holiday some years later was spent near Gairloch on the north-west coast of Scotland, opposite the Isle of Skye. The cottage where we were to stay was isolated and lay in a small bay. We had driven nearly thirty miles from the nearest railway station and were put down on the road with our big baskets of linen and table silver, until we could get a cart to take our baggage across the strip of sand to the cottage on the other side. From Gairloch we visited Skye. We also made many a climb under the guidance of our Scottish host, as he swung along, his kilt and sporran swaying to the rhythm of his long strides. And then there was Cornwall! We stayed in the Lizard village and walked every day along the narrow paths on the top of the low stone walls between cornfields, over which small blue butterflies hovered, to Kynance Cove. There we stayed all day long, or exploring the many beautiful pools among the rocks. At one o'clock we met for lunch at the one cottage in the cove. How good it tasted! The bread spread with jam and thick Cornish cream on top. Mother read aloud for a time after lunch, while we rested, before going off again to play or explore until it was time to walk back to the Lizard.

Hand in hand, Mother and Father would go off together, to walk along the high cliffs or to sit and talk or read together, while the cries from gulls from the Gull Rock, filled the air. On Sundays, on all our holidays, we attended the nearest church or chapel. Sometimes Father was asked to speak and in Switzerland it had happened more than once that Edith played the organ and we other girls would form a Quaker choir to lead the singing!

All our holidays had a certain rhythm. There were no cars or coaches, bringing large companies of trippers and we ourselves hardly ever went for an excursion. The days passed quietly and happily. We learned to know and love our surroundings, and there was time for peace and quiet to sink into us. It takes almost too much space to tell of these holiday experiences, but they formed an important part of Mother's life, and as such cannot be left out in the story of her life.

Grandfather John Cadbury died in 1889, before we left Moseley Hall. Some time later Auntie Maria married Joseph Fairfax and they went to live for some years at Boulogne-sur-Mer in France. Visits to Boulogne were a new and exciting experience; the boat journey from Dover to Calais and then by train to the little fishing-town, where the wives of the fishermen of the fishing-fleet waved goodbye to their husbands, wearing their wide frilled caps and picturesque costumes. We sometimes went to a small restaurant by the railway line, to watch the express train thunder past from Calais to Paris. That train carried the whole family a year or two later to Paris and Switzerland.

In Switzerland, Father and Mother, with their five daughters, spent several weeks, visiting places which Father knew and loved from the time when he was a young man, and with a guide walked and climbed among the mountains and valleys. There was a dramatic meeting with the old guide, when they embraced one another, overcome by the unexpected meeting! Bern, Lucerne, the Rigi, the Riffel Alp and Mürren were all visited. We climbed the Breithorn, and one excursion was made from Mürren to the St. Theodule Pass, from where we could look down into Italy. It had snowed not long before, and a great glacier was covered with the newly fallen soft snow. 'Walk lightly and stick your alpine stick deep in the snow', our guide warned, so as to avoid possible hidden crevasses!

A cold wind was blowing, and oh! How good the hot chocolate tasted in the little hut on top of the pass! On the way back I got so tired (I was 8 years old) struggling through the soft snow, that our guide took me on his back for a time!

In the spring of 1896 my Mother and Father visited Italy. On that journey they were accompanied by Jessie and Edith and myself. The others were working at school or college. We visited Milan and Florence, Rome and Naples. Father wrote to his absent children about the wonders of Naples and the near-by Pompeii, where excavating was in full swing. The lava pieces were picked out for visitors and a coin pressed into the glowing fluid lava. Innumerable museums were visited in Rome and Florence. My father wrote to Richard, who had just arrived in South Africa, where he was to begin fruit farming: March 24th, 1896. 'We have been hard at work among the beauty of the Italian lakes. We saw, in Milan, the original picture of Leonardo da Vinci, 'The Last Supper'; and then on to Rome with its treasures of the past ... Here we are now among the beautiful work of the men that made Florence: Michaelangelo, Dante, Savonarola, Galileo and Della Robbia and other great men.'

Those who had been left at home and also Auntie Maria were kept regularly in touch with our doings. My father's enthusiasm and keen interest in all he saw, was infectious, so that Mother and we daughters shared with him in all the new interests which were opened up for us. We were made aware through him, of the beauties of the landscape, of flowers and trees and of wonders of art, and glimpses into the history of past ages. No wonder that these holidays brought with them a richness of experience, which united us all more closely than ever.

EGYPT AND PALESTINE

In the early months of 1897, Richard and Emma and their four daughters set out for the longed for journey to Egypt and Palestine.

Thomas Cook had not long begun to arrange trips by steamboat up the Nile and camping tours through Palestine.

My father, who had read and studied much about Egypt and Palestine infected his wife and daughters with his enthusiasm and longing to see the wonders of the pyramids and old temples. The journey was made by train through France and Italy, to Brindisi. My father was a bad sailor and his heart was not strong. The journey from Brindisi to Port Said (by P. And O. Boat), was the shortest voyage possible, lasting only about four or five days.

Port Said was our first contact with the East and the Arabs came swarming on board to carry our luggage, or sell embroideries or carpets, jewelry [sic] *and other things, which they pressed upon us and wanted us to buy.*

To Cairo we travelled by train and stayed there in Shepard's [sic] *Hotel. From the front terrace of the hotel we could watch the crowds that thronged the streets; Arabs and many other nationalities, open carriages, donkeys and mules.*

From Cairo we drove out by carriage to the Pyramids and the Sphinx. We had hardly time to step out of the carriage, before being seized by two Arabs and dragged up the great stones of which the Pyramid is built, to the top. Now and again they asked: 'I make you satisfied?' and when we answered in the affirmative they would say: 'You make me satisfied when we come down.' Later we were pulled, sometimes almost crawling along the narrow hot passages of the Great Pyramid, to the bare central room where a large empty sarcophagus stood. We rode on camels, to where at that time only the great head of the Sphinx showed above the sand, the mysterious gaze of the eyes looking out over the desert.

I often think with what excited interest both my mother and father would have heard of the finding and excavating of the Tempel [sic] *of the Sphinx, and the finding of the tomb of Tutankhamun* [sic] *with all its treasures.*

The journey up the Nile was made on Cook's steamer, the Rameses II. *We were (as I remember it) a group of forty to fifty people on board. Our dragoman – Raschild – accompanied us and every evening told us about the temple or tombs which we were to visit next day; he invariably ended with 'And don't forget to remember your monument tickets.'*

APPENDIX II

From day to day we journeyed up the brown waters of the Nile, passing the white-winged sailing boats and, on either side, small villages and cultivated fields, with peasants often drawing up water from the river to pour into narrow channels through the fields, to water their crops.

In this way we visited Adfu, Karnac, Thebes and the tombs of the Kings, Luxor, Edu and Assuan. At Assuan the Nile flowed then over the first cataract to a lower level, and in the middle of the river was the tree shaded island of Philae with many beautiful temples.

After this journey up the Nile and back to Cairo, the party went by boat to Jaffa in Palestine. We cast anchor behind the rocky barrier which surrounds the harbour, and before long, small boats arrived into which we stepped and were owed ashore, waiting for a wave to carry us though a narrow opening between the rocks into the calmer waters beyond. In Jaffa, we had our first glimpse of the orange groves. How delicious the oranges tasted as we picked them ripe from the trees!

From Jaffa we drove in two open carriages the two days' journey to Jerusalem. The night was spent in a little German hotel in Ramleh and continued through the Judaean hills until the walls of the ancient city came into sight. I shall never forget what a moment of deep emotion this was for my father and mother, and indeed for us all.

We stayed in the Grand (now Imperial) Hotel, just inside the Jaffa Gate, not far from Mount Zion. Our dragoman, Ghalil Gandour, who was to accompany us on a camping tour, met us here. With him we visited the many historical sites in and around Jerusalem. On horseback we rode to Hebron, Jericho and the Dead Sea. A bathe in the Dead Sea was an experience, for we could stand upright half out of the water. We were glad to wash off the salt a little later in the fresh water of the fords of the Jordan.

After our return to Jerusalem, the real camping tour began, which was to take us through many places of historical and religious interest, right up to Damascus.

We had three sleeping tents and a kitchen and a dining tent. These were packed day by day on the backs of mules and went ahead to be ready to welcome us on a new site in the evening. Our horses had, of course, all Biblical names – Jacob, David, Gabriël, Beelzebub, Adam. The start was made in stormy weather. We had not got very far from Jerusalem when a violent hail-storm overtook us and while it lasted the horses turned tail and refused to go further. That night our tents had been set up in Bethel. The ground was a pool of mud, and rain and thunder storms continued all night. In spite of everything our cook, who was with us all through the trip, managed to make a wonderful hot dinner on his open brazier. This unhappy inauspicious beginning had one very happy result. As the weather the following morning was no better, we decided to seek refuge in a Latin monastery in the nearby town of Ramallah. In Ramallah was a girls' school, carried on by the American Friends' Missionary Society. We were given a warm welcome, and Father and Mother were especially interested to see the school and to attend the Sunday morning meeting.

When the storm was over, our party set out again; along footpaths over the hills and through the valleys. A small tent was taken with us for lunch, while we rested or visited some place of special interest.

I can remember sitting on the low wall of a deep well, which was supposed to be the well where Jesus talked with the woman of Samaria, and gazing out over the wild plain of Esdraelon.

When we reached the lake of Galilee and had set up our camp near the hot springs, not far from Tiberias, rain and storm overtook us again. Once more we sought refuge in a monastery, this time one belonging to the Greek Orthodox Church. We were welcomed and set up our camp in the monastery. The monks were interested in their unexpected guests and Father had several long talks with one of them.

We did not leave before going out in a boat on the lake and bathing in the nearly boiling hot springs, followed by a swim in the cooler waters of the lake.

When our journey was continued we followed the course of the Jordan to one of its sources. Chalil warned us to ride close together and keep very quiet, for the hill people of that district were often at enmity with strangers. Indeed, at one place some stones were thrown at us, but we passed on without further trouble and followed our paths over the lower slopes of Hermon, until in the distance the walls of Damascus came into sight. In Damascus we visited several places of interest and from there went to the wonderful ruins of the Temple of Baalbek and saw the quarry where one giant stone still lies on its way to the Temple!

At that time Father's first cousin, Caroline Cadbury was working in Brummana above Beirut in the Friends' Mission Station, and Father particularly wanted to visit her there. If I remember rightly, the journey from Damascus to Beirut was made by train. From there open carriages took us the four hours' journey to Brummana, first through orange groves, and later zigzagging up the steep road between the olive groves and through small villages.

The mission station of the F.F.M.A. consisted of the Girls' Training Home, and a hospital. Cousin Carrie welcomed us warmly and also the other missionaries, including Dr. Beshara Manasseh and his wife Rosa, then living in their hospitable home in Roisey. The view far out over the Mediterranean sea and along the coast line north and south was most beautiful. Sometimes too, the tops of the mountains of Cyprus were silhouetted against the sunset. Far below the tiny specks of fishing boats, fishing for sponges, were visible, and at night the twinkling lights of Beirut.

This was a fitting end to this memorable journey and we returned to England, once again by way of Port Said and Brindisi.

[...]

THE LONELY JOURNEY
The journey to Egypt and Palestine had been so full of interest, that it was decided to repeat it two years later and to extend it this time by going by boat to the second cataract

of the Nile, so that we could see the great temple of Abu Simbil and other interesting sites.

Edith's husband [by this time], Arnold Butler, was this time to be one of the party. Their little son Dickie (Richard Cadbury Butler) who had been born the year before, was to stay with his Butler grandparents.

As before, the journey up the Nile was made by steamer, visiting the same places. At Assuan, by the first cataract, we changed into a second steamer for the further journey. It was indeed a privilege to see the wonderful temple of Abu Simbil on its original site, the great seated figures of the Pharaohs, their hands open upon their knees, gazing out across the water.

On the way back to Cairo we visited the American Mission Station at Assiut. All unknowing, several of our party became infected with diphtheria, and became ill in Shepard's Hotel in Cairo.

My father and Helen had it very badly, but when the doctor assured them that they were well enough to travel, the journey was continued to Jerusalem, and all hoped that the same camping tour as two years earlier could be carried out. Alas this was not to be so – my father's heart was not strong and the journey from Cairo, so soon after his illness, had been too great a strain.

We stayed in the same hotel as on the former occasion near the Jaffa Gate. We had not been there many days, when in the early hours of the 22nd of March, we were called to my father's bedside, where he lay unconscious after a heart attack. He did not regain consciousness and passed away soon after.

We stood by my mother at the bedside. Twenty seven years of ideal unity had been theirs. Now Mother stood desolate, with the lonely years stretching out before her.

Dr. Wheeler, who was working at that time in the Hospital for the Jews in Jerusalem, had been called in. His warm sympathy and advice was a great help. My father's body was removed to the hospital, while the many arrangements had to be made for the return journey.

My father had wished to be buried in the comparatively new cemetery of Lodge Hill, in Selly Oak; and it was my mother's desire to carry out this expressed wish.

During the strange, unreal hours of the days that followed, again and again, the bells of a nearby church played the melody of the hymn:

> *Thy way, not mine, O Lord.*
> *However dark it be,*
> *Oh, lead me by Thine own right hand,*
> *Choose Thou the path for me.*

> *Not mine, not mine, the choice,*
> *In things or great or small:*
> *Be Thou to me my Guide, my Strength,*
> *My Wisdom and my All.*

Appendix III

Not everyone was happy with what the good Richard Cadbury and those like him were doing. However, a more positive reflection appeared in one of the daily papers in February 1893, under the heading 'Adult Sunday Schools in Birmingham'. This gives a good first person account of how the classes were conducted. (Reproduced from *Richard Cadbury of Birmingham*.)

The largest of these, and perhaps the most highly organised, is Class XV. of the Severn Street School – a branch which is under the superintendence and fostering of Mr. Richard Cadbury in the Moseley Road Schools. A kindly invitation to visit this school came at an opportune moment. Though it entailed unusually early rising, I sat down at seven o'clock to breakfast in one of the class-rooms with the teachers, a pleasant, unconstrained gathering over which Mr. Cadbury, the host, presided. This gentleman has for years set an example of punctuality and regularity of attendance at the school, and has ever been foremost in initiating or aiding all its various useful institutions. Breakfast over, a move was made to the main schoolroom, where the pupils were gathered together to open the proceedings with a hymn, followed by a short Bible reading and a prayer by Mr. Cadbury. Then they bustled off to their various classrooms, to sit down to their copybooks, their writing from dictation, or in copying verses of Scripture, or in the reading classes. Very diligent and painstaking pupils they all were. No need for sharp reproofs or calls to order. Anything savouring of coercion would be fatal at once. A strongly marked feature of the whole gathering was its thoroughly democratic spirit. Discipline in the ordinary sense of the term there was none; yet there was perfect order. The term "schoolmaster" would be out of place, because there is no sense of mastership. Teacher is the word, whether for the superintendent of the school or for the junior member of the teaching staff. Here is fully realised the doctrine which is usually but a theory, of the "brotherhood of man," the essence of true socialism and of true religion. The relationship in which the teacher stands to the pupil is most aptly likened to that of an elder brother. Doubtless this harmonious state of things was not produced at the outset; it has been evolved by experience. "Sanctified common sense" has taught those who are working in this great movement the right means of reaching the men at whose welfare they are aiming. The teachers have learned to understand and to appreciate the spirit of their pupils. It is no wonder that at first the young men who diffidently undertook the work shrank from the difficulties which inexperienced men would anticipate in dealing with a school of grown men of the roughest type – those who had been always regarded as the class least amenable to law and order. But trust in the men themselves has been the principle which has led to success. There is no desire on the part of the pupils to break from the routine of the establishment, and the work upon which each man is engaged is not a task, but a labour of love. It is a sight indeed affording food for satisfaction to see great rugged-faced men, with their hands stiffened by their daily toil, earnestly labouring over the letters they are putting together in their copy-books [sic]. *They all came cleanly and respectably dressed, and on the secretary being asked whether the men always looked so respectable, "Not when many of them first came," was the reply; "but they never attend long before a marked improvement is to be seen in their appearance. They soon become more careful about the condition of their clothes and about personal cleanliness. We have actually had them come here, occasionally, under the influence of liquor." "And do you turn them away when they come in that state?" was the natural question to ask.*

"Oh, no; we let them sit down with the rest, and do our best with them; but we have to use great care and patience."
"Are you able to say that you have reclaimed permanently any habitual drunkards, because some people contend that such men are never really reclaimed?" "Yes, we have a class almost full of such men there (pointing to the class-rooms). It is the drunkards' class, and the teacher you see there instructing them was himself once a great drunkard. He had now been for many years a most consistent and earnest Christian man, and his success with men who have given way to drink is remarkable."

Further Reading

Bibliography

A History of Cadbury Wordsworth, Diane (Pen & Sword, Barnsley, November, 2018)

Barrow Cadbury Bartlett, Percy W. (Bannisdale Press, London, 1960)

Beatrice: The Cadbury Heiress Who Gave Away Her Fortune Joseph, Fiona (Foxwell Press, Birmingham, 2012)

Birmingham Snow Hill: a first class return Harrison, Derek (Peter Watts Publishing, Woodchester, 1986)

Birmingham Weekly Mercury (1899)

Cadbury Brothers Limited: A Brief Record of the Founders and their Successors to the Present Day Cadbury Brothers Ltd (Bournville, 1968)

Cocoa – all about it by "Historicus" (private edition, 1896)

Elizabeth Cadbury Scott, Richenda C. (Harrap, London, 1955)

Cadbury's Angels: Memories of working with George Cadbury from Bridge Street to Bournville Carrington, Iris (Monks Bridge Books, 2011)

Emma Richard Cadbury: 1846 – 1907 Boeke, Beatrice C. (private edition)

Gospel Temperance Herald (17 May 1882)

John Cadbury: 1801 – 1889 Insull, Tom (private edition, Birmingham, 1979)

Life of George Cadbury Gardiner, A.G. (Cassell and Company Limited, London, 1923)

Poems by Richard Cadbury Cadbury Alexander, Helen – compiled by (privately published, date unknown)

Private family correspondence and letters (various dates)

Richard Cadbury of Birmingham Cadbury Alexander, Helen (Hodder & Staughton, London, 1906)

Richard Tapper Cadbury: 1768 – 1860 Cadbury, William A. (private edition, Birmingham, 1944)

The Book of Christian Discipline of the Religious Society of Friends (1883)

The Firm of Cadbury: 1831 – 1931 Williams, Iolo A. (Constable and Co Ltd, London, 1931)

The Moseley Society Journal, Vol 1, No 5 (1894)

William A. Cadbury: 1867 – 1957 (private edition, 1958)

Books

A History of the Cadbury Family Crosfield John F. CBE DSc MA (London, 1985)

Two Brothers and a Chocolate Factory Bell, Juliet Clare (author) and Mikhail, Jess (illustrator) (Bournville Village Trust, Birmingham, 2016)

Websites

A History of Birmingham Places and Placenames from A to Y: https://billdargue.jimdo.com/placenames-gazetteer-a-to-y/places-r/rotton-park/ (Rotton Park)

BBC History: http://www.bbc.co.uk/history/british/victorians/famine_01.shtml (The Irish Famine)

BBC Legacies: http://www.bbc.co.uk/legacies/myths_legends/england/birmingham/article_3.shtml (Talking Tolkien)

Birmingham City Council: https://www.birmingham.gov.uk/info/20089/parks/406/lickey_hills_country_park (The Lickey Hills)

Birmingham City Council: https://www.birmingham.gov.uk/reservoir (Edgbaston Reservoir)

Birmingham Conservation Trust: http://www.birminghamconservationtrust.org/our-projects/bct-finished/perrotts-folly/ (Perrott's Folly)

BirminghamLive: https://www.birminghammail.co.uk/news/midlands-news/hidden-spaces-edgbaston-waterworks-inspiration-10645055 (Edgbaston Waterworks)

British History Online: https://www.british-history.ac.uk (OS Map 013/12)

FURTHER READING

CPI Inflation Calculator: https://www.in2013dollars.com/uk/inflation/ 1890

Edgbaston Golf Club: https://www.edgbastongc.co.uk/history (History)

Historic UK: https://www.historic-uk.com/HistoryMagazine/Destinations UK/Malvern/ (Malvern)

History: https://www.history.com/topics/immigration/irish-potato-famine (Irish Potato Famine)

Parks & Gardens: https://www.parksandgardens.org/places/edgbaston-hall (Edgbaston Hall)

TimeOut Birmingham: https://www.timeout.com/birmingham/blog/ how-birmingham-inspired-j-r-r-tolkien (J.R.R. Tolkien)

Uffculme Centre: http://www.theuffculmecentre.co.uk (The Uffculme Centre)

Wikipedia: https://en.wikipedia.org/wiki/Moseley_Hall,_Birmingham (Moseley Hall)

Woodbrooke Quaker Conference Centre: https://www.woodbrooke.org. uk (Woodbrooke College)

About the Author

Diane Wordsworth was born and bred in Solihull in the West Midlands when it was still Warwickshire. She started to write for magazines in 1985 and became a full-time freelance photo-journalist in 1996. In 1998, she became sub-editor for several education trade magazines and started to edit classroom resources, textbooks and non-fiction books.

In 2004 Diane moved from the Midlands to South Yorkshire where she edited an in-house magazine for an international steel company for six years. She still edits and writes on a freelance basis.

Catch up with Diane today

Website: www.dianewordsworth.com
Facebook page: www.facebook.com/DMWordsworth/
Twitter: @DMWordsworth
LinkedIn: www.linkedin.com/in/dianewordsworth

Books by Diane Wordsworth

Fiction
Night Crawler: a Marcie Craig Mystery

Short story collections

Twee Tales
Twee Tales Too

Writers' guides

Diary of a Scaredy Cat: a year in the life of a frightened writer

History books

A History of Cadbury

Index